Boris, Boats and Me: Creating Memorable Guest Experiences at Chester Zoo

(Illustrated)

Paul Woods

ISBN: 9798613168071

DEDICATION

This book is dedicated to my friends and colleagues in the Guest Experience team at Chester Zoo who helped to make creating memorable experiences for others such a worthwhile experience for me.
Any royalties from the sale of this book will be donated to Chester Zoo.

CONTENTS

Acknowledgements   i

1 Fire ravages the Monsoon Forest   1

2 The origins of zoos   7

3 Guest experience at Chester Zoo   14

4 The chimp family   31

5 George Mottershead and his family 38

6 Our Zoo – the drama   49

7 Break-ins and breakouts   55

8 Lanterns, bugs and predators   65

9 Visitor attractions   87

10 The Secret Life of the Zoo   108

11 Keeping the staff happy   115

12 Keeping the animals happy   122

13 Preventing extinction   127

14 Dealing with Coronavirus   130

ACKNOWLEDGEMENTS

I am grateful to colleagues at the zoo who contributed ideas and suggestions for this book.

CHAPTER ONE: FIRE RAVAGES THE MONSOON FOREST

It was a pretty miserable December day. The sky was dull and overcast, the weather forecast rain, and it was quite windy. I wasn't particularly looking forward to setting off to Chester Zoo at half past one in time for my four-hour shift that afternoon. On bright sunny days, even in mid-winter, it was always a delight to arrive at the zoo knowing that, in between whatever tasks I had been assigned to that day, I would be out in the fresh air, enjoying the winter sun, getting plenty of exercise and taking a few moments to observe any animals I came across in the course of my part-time job as a Guest Experience assistant.

Around noon I strolled down the road to the local newsagents in Handbridge to buy a morning paper. I remarked to the sales assistant behind the counter, "What a miserable day. I'm not looking forward to working at the zoo this afternoon."

"I don't think you will be," he replied. "Take a look at

this." He showed me a video on his mobile phone of the monsoon forest at the zoo, with flames shooting out of the roof and smoke billowing upwards hundreds of feet into the air, driven by the strong wind.

I'd left my mobile behind and hurried back to the house to check for myself what was going on. I called the supervisor's mobile. "I've just seen pictures of the zoo on fire. Should I come into work as usual at two o'clock?"

"No, we're evacuating everyone, so you'd better take the day off and check back again early tomorrow morning."

The Monsoon Forest was one of the star attractions on the Islands, a £40 million project to develop a new area of the zoo which had opened in mid-2015. The largest indoor habitat in the UK, it allowed birds and small animals to roam about freely in a large area planted with lush tropical vegetation and kept at a constant 26 degrees. According to the zoo website, "During 2013 the building phase of the Islands project began. Islands (is) a brand-new experience at Chester Zoo, where visitors will be able to embark on a unique expedition to discover six different south east Asian island habitats. The experience will showcase the wonderful stories of the special biodiversity of South East Asian islands and the zoo's involvement in protecting that biodiversity through our animal breeding and in-country field programmes." [1] The second phase of the Islands project, Monsoon Forest, was launched in July 2015. This featured its own tropical weather system and a variety of tropical plant species. In addition to the Sulawesi crested macaque, rhinoceros hornbill, Asian forest tortoise and the tentacled snake, Monsoon Forest was home to two Sunda gharial crocodiles in a special enclosure which incorporated an underwater viewing area. Also included were raised walkways and free flight areas for the enclosure's birds.

Colleagues who were working at the zoo had graphic stories to tell of how the alarm was sounded around 11.20 when fire broke out inside the monsoon forest area. The number one priority was to ensure the safety and welfare of all the guests, including any who were at risk of smoke inhalation. Then came the welfare and safety of the animals whose habitat was going up in flames. Initially the precise cause of the fire was the subject of speculation, but it was eventually established that it was started by an electrical fault. In the hot tropical atmosphere inside the vast polymer-covered domed roof of the Monsoon Forest, it spread rapidly and very quickly got completely out of control.

The zoo's crisis management system swung into action as thick black smoke was blown by the wind across the Islands. Guests were quickly directed off the Islands and towards the exits, passengers on the Lazy River Boat Ride which skirts one side of the monsoon forest were hastily evacuated, and keepers were spotted heading towards the scene of the fire where, under the overall guidance of the firefighters, they desperately attempted to evacuate as many of the animals trapped inside the burning enclosure as possible. It is a miracle that none of the visitors or staff was seriously injured. A major incident was declared, attended by 15 fire engines from three different counties. Sadly, the fire killed about a dozen birds and smaller species such as frogs, fish and stick insects, but zoo staff managed to save all the larger mammals including the critically endangered Sumatran orangutans, Sulawesi macaque monkeys and endangered silvery gibbons as well as large reptiles like the Asian forest tortoise and also the two crocodiles which had remained safely under water. Friends of the zoo started a crowd-funding page and had raised £50,000 within a matter of days, with the final total reaching over £260,000.

Fortunately, the multi-million-pound cost of restoring the Monsoon Forest was covered by insurance and the money raised by friends of the zoo went to provide additional support for the zoo's conservation projects around the world. The steel trusses supporting the roof were removed to be shot-blasted and repainted during 2019, and the huge polymer dome has been replaced to ensure a hot and humid environment when the animals are eventually allowed back in.

Contractors at work on the Monsoon Forest

"Cheshire Live" reported that the soil and subsoil inside the domed building had to be replaced and everything washed down to prevent any contamination from the plastic roof which had melted onto the ground below.[2] Temporary homes for the rescued species were found around the zoo - the orangutans, for example, returned to their previous habitat in the Realm of the Red Ape - and in November 2019 Sumatran orangutan Subis, one of the many animals which had been led to safety, gave birth there to a healthy baby.

ENDNOTES

1   Downloaded on 14.1.2020 from https://www.chesterzoo.org/memories/building-work-starts-on-our-islands-project/

2   Downloaded on 14.1.2020 from https://www.cheshire-live.co.uk/news/chester-cheshire-news/chester-zoos-monsoon-forest-rises-17388783

CHAPTER 2: THE ORIGINS OF ZOOS

Wild animals were first kept in captivity in China and Egypt as long ago as the fourth and fifth millennia BC. Wealthy citizens, aristocrats and rulers kept wild animals to show off their wealth and power. By the sixteenth century the Portuguese, Spanish, French and English began exploring the globe and often brought back exotic animals and birds which were kept as pets or put on show by the rich and wealthy.

The first zoos emerged in the 19th century as public collections managed by professional staff, replacing private animal collections and menageries. The Jardin de Plantes in Paris was the first example of a collection intended to serve an entire nation rather than royalty and the aristocracy. Following the French Revolution, animals from displays on public highways and princely menageries were moved to the Jardin des Plantes where they were put on display for the enjoyment of all the people.

By the late 19th century there were zoos in most major European cities. The London Zoological Gardens was established in 1828 in Regent's Park, followed by zoos in Dublin (1831) and Bristol (1835), whilst in the United States zoos began to appear after the Civil War, with the first one opening in Philadelphia in 1868.

A lot has been written about the history of zoos and the science of looking after animals. Cultural attitudes to keeping and caring for animals in captivity change rapidly. In the last century people flocked to see animals in cages. Animal shows entertained visitors in circuses and animal fights showed the strength of the beasts. During the era of colonial expansion in the second half of the 19th century, the strength and wealth of the colonial powers was demonstrated by the display of new and seemingly extraordinary animals found in distant places.[1] The history of the development of zoos shows how public attitudes have changed over time. Mahatma Gandhi acutely observed that "the greatness of a nation and its moral progress can be judged by the way its animals are treated."

According to Peter Singer, "To seek to reduce the suffering of those who are completely under one's domination, and unable to fight back, is truly a mark of a civilized society. Charting the progress of animal-welfare legislation around the world is therefore an indication of moral progress more generally". [2]

In 2011 the British Parliament passed a motion directing the government to ban the use of wild animals in circuses. PETA argued over the next decade that "forcing wild animals to perform confusing tricks is a barbaric practice that has no place in a compassionate society. Wild animals used in travelling circuses are carted from one venue to another in cramped cages and barren trailers and are taught to perform tricks through the threat of punishment." [3]

Finally after almost a decade of debate and campaigning, the use of wild animals in circuses in the UK was banned from 2020. At times, however, it has seemed that gains for animals in Western countries have been outweighed by increasing animal abuse in other countries such as China, as growing prosperity there boosts demand for animal products. Sickening footage available online shows bears kept in cages so small that they cannot stand up, or in some cases move at all, so that bile can be taken from them. Worse still (if one can compare such atrocities) is a video showing fur-bearing animals being skinned alive and thrown onto a pile of other animals, where they are left to die slowly. Long before Western philosophers included animals in their ethics, Chinese philosophers like Zhuangzi said that love should permeate relations not only between humans, but between all sentient beings. Nowadays, China has its own animal-rights campaigners, and there are signs that their message is beginning to be heard.

One recent sign of progress in China relates to animal performances. Chinese zoos have drawn crowds by staging animal spectacles, and by allowing members of the public to buy live chickens, goats, and horses in order to watch them being pulled apart by lions, tigers, and other big cats. Now the Chinese government has forbidden state-owned zoos from taking part in such cruelty. Singer argues, "The best hope for further progress, it seems, lies in animal welfare becoming, like human rights, an international issue that affects countries' reputations." [4]

According to Gray, "A well-run modern zoo is a zoo that uses the best available knowledge and technology to make evidence-based decisions, listens to public sentiment and is committed to animals as individuals and as species. Well-run zoos inform public views, leading the expansion of the knowledge of animals and the environment and at all times demonstrating a respectful way of treating animals, people and the environment…The welfare and care of the animals receives as much attention as business operations or visitor services. A focus on conservation and the dedication of zoos to transform into conservation organisations results in the benefits of zoo operations flowing beyond the zoo walls." [5]

Since the 19th century, zoos have evolved from menagerie type collections into conservation centres. "Menageries" were old-fashioned zoos that were designed to display as many species as possible. Most animals were not bred in captivity but taken directly from the wild and were displayed in small cages, without much consideration for the welfare of the animals. Nowadays zoos aim to educate their visitors about the living world, ensuring that every visitor is aware of the importance of nature conservation. The animals in zoos and aquaria serve as ambassadors for animals in the wild and inspire visitors to care for and understand natural ecosystems and the threats that these systems face. Many of the visitors to zoos are children, who are the future caretakers of the planet. At the zoo, they can develop a larger sense of respect and understanding towards the living world. An effective way of educating visitors is ensuring that they have a really great and memorable day out! This ensures the visitors remember what they have seen or learnt.

This department in Cedar House appears to be staffed 24/7

Zoos educate their visitors by displaying animals in good exhibits that cater for their physical and psychological needs. Signs, exhibitions and educators serve to teach the visitors about the animals and the habitat they live in. Animals are stimulated to show their most natural behaviour by providing them with environmental enrichment and through good enclosure design. Zoos in the 21st century acknowledge the need to conserve biodiversity. Mankind cannot foresee the after-effects of collapsing ecosystems; therefore zoos aim to support a large range of conservation efforts. Many plant and animal species are threatened with extinction due to human activities. Zoos highlight flagship species - charismatic animals that represent an ecosystem, the conservation of which would protect the future of less charismatic species that share the habitat. One way in which zoos and aquaria contribute to the continued survival of species is by managing their populations in ex-situ breeding programmes. They aim to provide the highest standards of animal care and husbandry. In addition to this, research conducted in zoos is vital for conservation and the understanding of biodiversity. [6]

In 1999 the Council of the European Union (EU) adopted the "Zoos Directive" which provides measures for member states to implement the licensing and inspection of zoos. The directive states that zoos in the European Union will:

• Participate in conservation research
• Promote public awareness on conservation
• Have proper accommodation and care for animals
• Assure safety for animals

- Maintain adequate animal records
- Participate in captive breeding where appropriate
- Participate in conservation training. [7]

Most zoos have vision and mission statements. Chester Zoo's mission statement has evolved over time. In 2006 it was "To be a major force in conserving biodiversity worldwide." By 2020 this had become simply, "Our mission is preventing extinction."

ENDNOTES

1   Gray, J (2017) Zoo Ethics: The Challenges of Compassionate Conservation. CSIRO Publishing, Ithaca, p14.

2   Singer, P. Moral Progress and Animal Welfare. Downloaded on 22.1.2020 from https://www.abc.net.au/religion/moral-progress-and-animal-welfare/10101318

3   Downloaded from https://www.peta.org.uk/blog/england-circus-victory/

4   Singer, P ibid

5   Gray (2017) ibid, p 36

6   Downloaded on 21.1.2020 from https://www.eaza.net/assets/Uploads/images/Membership-docs-and-images/Zoo-Management-Manual-compressed.pdf p 9

7   ibid p10

CHAPTER 3: GUEST EXPERIENCE AT CHESTER ZOO

"Want to work in Guest Experience at Chester Zoo? Here's a peek behind the scenes…" So goes the title of a short promotional clip posted by the zoo on YouTube. [1]

"We need to make sure that customers get the best experience that they can," asserts one of the Guest Experience staff. "That's what it's all about – creating a truly memorable experience for our guests."

Scott Manton, one of the Supervisors, adds: "We make sure we have staff who are on hand to help out and make an enjoyable day for everyone who comes." Other staff reinforce this message: "It's all about making the zoo the best place for our guests." "If you're working in the guest experience department, definitely come prepared!"

Scott goes on to say, "When it's raining and when it's cold, you've got all that work to do still. You still have to be in the moment, and it can be quite hard. The top tip would be to remember that you're part of the experience."

Other staff members add,

"We pick up litter, clean toilets, we brush things, clean

bird poo off signs for visitors."

"Make the most of every day, that you're being positive, happy all the time."

"Interact with as many customers as you can and see as many animals as you can each day."

"The environment that we work in is just amazing. There's no other job where you can be in a meeting, and then the next minute you're outside and you see a rhino or a giraffe…"

Scott has the final word at the end of the short clip, "Look where you work, and if that doesn't get you through the day, nothing will."

I make a brief appearance in the video myself, pushing a tilt truck in the rain with a load of toilet rolls on the way to replenishing supplies in one of the washroom storerooms, blissfully unaware that I am being filmed.

The year I retired after thirty seven years spent working as a teacher trainer, English Language Teaching expert and cultural diplomat for The British Council, (the United Kingdom's international organisation for cultural relations and educational opportunities), I spent three months in total as part of a team advising Colleges of Excellence in Saudi Arabia on how best to improve the quality of English Language teaching in the thirty seven new technical and vocational training colleges which the Saudi government had set up at vast expense in all corners of the country. Half-way through the project, the team leader resigned at short notice, so I ended up writing the final report and recommendations. The money in Saudi was good - the fees were around £500 per day - but the quality of life as a consultant there was probably best suited to someone younger and more adaptable.

So early the following year I decided to look around for a part-time job closer to home which would keep me out of mischief. Two jobs caught my eye. One was as an English Language trainer, teaching on a six-week summer course in Manchester for Qatari policemen, the other as a Guest Experience Assistant at Chester Zoo. I polished my c.v. and sent off applications for both. The selection process for Manchester Metropolitan University involved teaching a class of students, a written exercise and an oral interview. I got the impression during the interview that they were looking for someone much younger, although as a former Director of the British Council's Peacekeeping English project for military, police and border guards I felt

I was very well-qualified for the job. The zoo's selection process involved a short written exercise and a fifteen-minute interview with Scott Manton. He appeared to be somewhat concerned that someone with my professional background might find it a bit infra dig to clean washrooms and empty litter bins. I tried to convince him that this wouldn't be a problem, quoting as an example the six months I had spent in between school and university as a hospital porter at the now demolished Leasowe Hospital, where occasionally one had to clean the visitor toilets and from time to time the job of emptying bins had involved taking plastic bags containing various body parts from outside the operating theatre to the incinerator and tossing them into the flames.

The zoo was fairly quick off the mark and offered me the job, which I accepted, then a few weeks later I got a rejection letter from MMU, so I had made the right decision. After tax the salary for a month would be not much more than I had earned in a day in Saudi, but I felt that it would be a much more rewarding environment to work in.

Following a day's induction course, held at Chester racecourse, I began working in Zone 2 at the zoo. For administrative purposes the zoo was divided into three zones, Zone 1 covering the area near the entrance and including the tills and admission gates, Zone 2 the far side of the public footpath which divides the zoo in half, and Zone 3 the newly-created Islands area. In Zone 2 we had many interesting enclosures, including the lions, penguins, chimpanzees, orangutans, giant otters, jaguars and sloths, to mention just a few.

The picture on the back cover – I wasn't actually in danger from the jaguars!

A close-up of spotted male Napo

I had only been working at the zoo for a few days when one of the keepers pointed out there was a Thomas the Tank Engine toy floating in the ditch at the edge of the giraffe enclosure. It was too far away to reach with a litter picker, so I went and got a very long litter picker which was kept at the monorail control room. The water in the ditch was very stagnant and the toy was covered in mud and slime. Our instructions were to take any lost property such as hats, bags, teddy bears and animal toys to Guest Services so they could potentially be reunited with the owners. However, I thought to myself, "No self-respecting parent is going to want to give that back to their offspring," and chucked it away in the nearest litter bin.

Standing outside the giraffe enclosure with a very long litter-picker

The next morning one of the Zone 2 Coordinators asked me, "You didn't by any chance find a Thomas the Tank Engine toy yesterday when you were on site clean, did you?"

"Funny you should ask me that," I replied. "I found one in the ditch by the giraffes, but it looked so disgusting that I threw it out!"

"Oh, you shouldn't have done that, it was the child's favourite toy," came the reply.

I felt so bad about it that, later that day when I was passing the now defunct Toys 'R Us in Chester's Greyhound Park, I popped in and asked if they had a

Thomas the Tank Engine. They did, and as it was only £4.99 and pretty much identical to the one which I'd thrown out, I bought it and handed it in to Guest Services the following day. I never did hear if it ever got reunited with its owner!

One of the jobs I liked best was "site clean" which often meant getting up early and working from 7 to 11, mostly before the zoo opened at 1000 a.m. Depending on the time of year, you could watch the sun rise and observe the animals feeding undisturbed by any visitors, just you and the odd keeper or security guard and otherwise not a soul about.

We were encouraged to interact proactively with the visitors, not waiting to be spoken to first. Sometimes we had to act like policemen, telling people off if they were doing something antisocial or just plain foolish. Zoos serve a dual purpose, being both a place to entertain children as well as an institution for conservation and environmental education. The zoo has a play policy which encourages respect for animals and learning about them through guided play.

One of the tasks, especially in autumn, included using a leaf blower to create piles of leaves which you then swept up and took to the compactor or piled up in a storage area for the zoo gardeners to use later as manure. There were a few areas which were out of bounds for leaf blowing, including the paths near the chimpanzee enclosure where the chimps were liable to throw rocks, sticks, or clumps of grass at you if you disturbed their peace and tranquility.

Leaf-blowing in autumn is like painting the Forth Bridge.
A couple of hours earlier there wasn't a leaf to be seen!

Thetravel website [2] points out some of the things which families should avoid doing, for the safety of themselves or the animals, including the following:

1. Tapping on the glass.

Imagine someone knocking on your windows when you are trying to relax at home. That is what it feels like for zoo animals when people tap on the glass. It can be very stressful for the animals.

2. Tossing coins into animal enclosures.

People sometimes think that if there is a pond or ditch, that means they can make a wish and throw a coin into it. This is a bad idea, because coins are small enough for the animals to eat and choke on. Coins can also be dangerous if the water that the animals drink absorbs nasty chemicals from the metal. In some zoos this is a major issue. An online article about Oklahoma City zoo [3] states the seal and sea lion pool has been a particular problem. Visitors have dropped coins, cell phones and even shoes in the pool.

"Historically it's always been a problem," Oklahoma City Zoo veterinarian Jennifer D'Agostino said. "When people see a body of water, they think it's a wishing well and want to throw in a coin."

The problem is that the seals and sea lions eat the coins. Pennies minted after 1982 are a particular problem because they have high levels of zinc, which breaks down easily inside an animal's stomach. The coins can cause kidney failure and liver problems. Loss of red blood cells and ulcers are another danger. The zoo lost Brindle, a 5-year-old harbour seal, in 2007 because she ingested 97 coins. Many of them were pennies.

3 Standing on enclosure walls or railings.

It may seem innocent to want to get a better view of the animals, but this is one of the most dangerous things you can do while visiting a zoo. In Chester Zoo there are warning signs, for example on bridges or walls with a steep drop, but there are many stories of children falling into animal enclosures in zoos around the world because a parent put them on the railing for a better view.

4 Throwing food or rubbish into animal enclosures.

Throwing any food into an animal enclosure in a zoo is an easy way to kill them. While it may seem entertaining to share your food with them, there are really tragic stories of zoo animals dying due to eating food that was poisonous for them. Animals have also died from eating rubbish thrown in their enclosures.

5 Making noises at animals to get their attention.

People often try to get the attention of the animals by making noises. Children howl at the wolves, growl at the tigers, and scream at the monkeys. This hardly ever works, as the animals are used to humans making strange noises and will ignore them. However, that doesn't stop the humans from making the noises which is annoying for other guests.

7 Not reading information and warning signs.

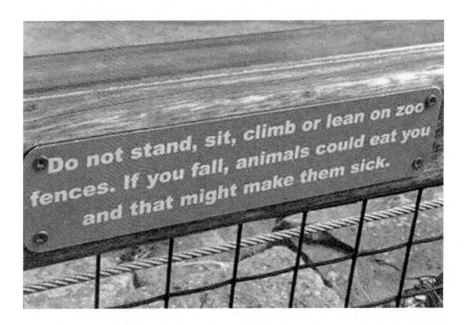

Zoos are filled with signs that show rules, regulations, and information. Signs do not always stop people, though. They either don't read them or just ignore them.

8. Touching the animals.

Only in petting zoos is touching the animals encouraged. Twenty years ago, Chester had a collection of goats, lambs and other tame animals near what is now Junes Restaurant, which children could pet, but not any longer. Just because there is no glass or cage between you and an animal does not mean you can touch the animal. In the new Madagascar enclosure at Chester, ring-tailed lemurs and other mammals are free to mingle with visitors, but it is never a good idea for children to try and touch them or they could get bitten.

9 Parents not watching their children closely.

Inevitably some children get separated from their parents. On a busy day this can happen several times in the course of a day. Lost children can be quickly reunited with their parents when a staff member informs Security who put out a call to all radios with a description of the lost child.

Sometimes the lost child can turn up very far away from where they were last seen. I remember one autistic lad who I reported was last seen near Junes Restaurant was found fifteen minutes later heading up the ramp into the Realm of the Red Ape, a good ten minutes' walk away! Apparently, he had also got lost on his previous visit to the zoo.

10 Smoking away from permitted smoking areas.

Chester Zoo is a no-smoking zone, but there are designated smoking areas dotted about, with cigarette bins, where smoking is permitted. Some guests, however, don't realise that the ban on smoking also includes vaping, and may get upset when asked not to vape outside the smoking areas.

One of the tasks we were required to do was emptying bins. This was fine for most of the year, but on a hot summer's day the bins filled up quickly, and ice cream cones and fizzy drinks attracted swarms of wasps. You were not supposed to kill these, but occasionally if they were particularly bad and no one was looking I was tempted to spray the bin with wasp-killer and wait a few minutes before replacing the bin bag. We were advised not to overfill the tilt trucks with bin bags. This was especially important during zoo opening hours when there were guests about, due to the risk of them falling off the truck. Once a tilt ruck was full, we would take them to various off-show locations around the zoo and empty them into large wheelie bins, ready for collection during the bin round later in the day.

Another task after very heavy rain was brushing puddles. There were some notorious spots which filled up even after relatively light downpours, including the path near the picnic lodge, close to the play area with tortoise shells, and the left turn into the overflow car park at the zoo entrance.

One of the most interesting training sessions was on using the different types of fire extinguisher. I learnt, amongst other things, that if operated incorrectly, Carbon

Puddle brushing

Fire extinguisher training

Dioxide (CO2) fire extinguishers come with a high risk associated to the user. Because the temperature is extremely low, using the device incorrectly can result in skin burns from long contact with the horn of the extinguisher, so you have to avoid holding it by this point.

Before the zoo opened or after it had closed for the day it was time for the bin round. If you didn't have a zoo licence, you assisted the driver, collecting bags of rubbish and loading these onto the back of a truck.

Black bags for general rubbish, blue bags for poo, white bags for cardboard, pink bags for nappies – it all goes in different directions as the zoo is very keen on recycling. It rained heavily the previous day and there was an awful lot of chimp poo!

If you were on the zoo premises during opening hours you had to walk in front of the truck to make sure it was safe for it to proceed at three or four miles an hour. The very first time I was on the bin round I pushed the sliding door on the side of the truck vigorously and nearly took the end off my finger, which got caught in the door. On another occasion the colleague who was driving got a good telling off when he approached a crowd of men in suits standing looking at the Madagascar play area.

How not to load a bin truck!

When they showed no sign of moving out of the road, he drove slowly past on the extreme left of the path but misjudged it and collided noisily with the overhanging branches of a tree.

ENDNOTES

1   Downloaded on 21.1.2020 from

https://www.youtube.com/watch?v=O2hshTLAQNc

2   Downloaded on 24.1.2020 from
https://www.thetravel.com/people-zoos-annoy-
staff/?fbclid=IwAR3u1EIHSYP6RqPW8n_HbxZuuvrI-
_C9CoSK-L8DlpAGPnMGhXTw-w9Ov58

3   Downloaded on 22.1.2020 from
https://oklahoman.com/article/5373405/coins-are-an-
ongoing-problem-for-oklahoma-city-zoo-veterinarian

CHAPTER 4: THE CHIMP FAMILY

The zoo family of twenty or so chimps in Chester includes an extraordinary character named Boris who has lived at the zoo for more than 50 years. The Wirral Globe recounts how Boris was hand reared by Hester Mundis in her New York apartment before handing him over to the zoo back in 1969. She had taken pity on him after spotting him as a frightened orphaned baby in a New York pet shop. Hester said, "Common sense didn't come into it. He looked so helpless and needed a 'mum'. I was already a working mother with an eight-year-old son and couldn't see what difference a chimp would make in our lives... Boris changed our lives completely. We raised him in our Manhattan apartment for nearly three years learning the hard and often hilarious way that what is normal behaviour in the jungle can be a disaster in an apartment! In 2004, when Boris was 38, Hester visited Boris at the zoo for the fourth time. Following the visit, she said, "I couldn't have wished more for Boris, as he has a wonderful life here. It was lovely to see him again. He was looking over to me in a puzzled way and taking a definite interest. I'd like to think he remembers me, but who knows." [1]

I was brushing up litter and leaves in the circular building which houses the chimpanzees one morning when one of them, I'm almost certain it was Boris, hurled his entire body with full force at one of the thick laminated glass sheets which separate the chimpanzees from visitors to the zoo.

"If he does that too often either he's going to cause himself a serious injury or the glass is going to shatter," I thought to myself.

Sure enough, a few days later, I discovered that the chimpanzee house had been closed to visitors and peering through the steel shutters at the entrance you could see that one of the huge glass sheets had a hole in one corner and the whole pane had shattered, although it was still firmly in place, looking like a shattered windscreen after it has been hit by a stone. It took several weeks before the glass could be replaced, and the chimpanzee house re-opened to the public again.

There are stories of how veteran chimp keeper Niall, who retired towards the end of 2019 after almost 50 years at the zoo, would bribe the chimps with bananas to give up any large sticks or stones they managed to uncover on their island enclosure lest they should throw them at passing visitors or staff.

In the fifth episode of the first series of Channel 4's "The Secret Life of the Zoo", Boris took a moorhen hostage and it was up to Niall – who has a long-term friendly bond with Boris, having known him since the chimp arrived at Chester Zoo in the late 1960s – to save the day. After beckoning Boris over to a door, Boris handed over the moorhen to Niall and was rewarded with some bread. [2]

Shortly after Boris Johnson became Prime Minister Prof. Howard Williams wrote an amusing blog post entitled "Back Boris":

"At the time of writing, it seems increasingly likely that the new Tory leader will be a charismatic but unprincipled and crooked chancer, with a demonstrable track record of incompetence and lying in public office. Many fear he will be driving the UK towards a Brexit that will be desirous only to the delusional and the xenophobic…Still, there is a way we can all 'Back Boris' right now and here's how.

I was at Chester Zoo today, enjoying the mammals, birds, fish and reptiles on show, as well as the animatronic predators from past ages, only to encounter a very charismatic Boris we all love. He is one not only far more worthy of public praise and support than the ex-Mayor of London, but perhaps one who certainly would do far less damage to the country if he was elected Prime Minster. To celebrate his 50th birthday in 2016, sculptor Gill Parker was commissioned to create a superb bronze of the noble beast. Situated outside the chimpanzee house, the bronze is placed on an oblong rough-hewn stone plinth. It is flanked by two boards. One explains the story of Boris: his early life, how he became an important member of the chimp community, and how he has inspired conservation through his mischief, his intelligence and his engaging personality.

The statue of Boris outside the Chimp house

Through his long-lived presence, and since 2016 enhanced by his beautiful statue, Boris is one of the most prominent and venerated 'animal ancestors' in Chester Zoo. He fits a pattern identified and discussed by contemporary archaeologist and heritage guru Professor Cornelius Holtorf for zoos elsewhere. Namely, human-like personalities in zoological gardens seem to be particularly afforded to elephants and apes, who take on a special prominence in both life and death as part of the zoo community. While death is denied in the zoo for most animals that dwell there, long-lived characters like Boris become significant foci of commemoration, not only representing their species, but the zoo more broadly and its entertainment and conservation dimensions.

Boris's 50th birthday present sculpture is not unique… yet the particular realism and spatial location of the bronze of Boris projects its significance and awaits the sad death of Boris himself. He is already installed in life as a venerated ancestor for the chimps and the zoo as a whole, integral to the landscape for visitors and a memorial for decades to come.

So come on, let's all back Boris in every regard, including for PM!" [3]

The chimpanzees also figured in the third series of "The Secret Life of the Zoo", where the focus was on being the newbie, sibling rivalry and feeling like the odd one out. *Cheshire Live* reported, "The attractive new girl in town who struggles to fit in is defended by the 'nice guy' but ends up ditching him in favour of the 'bad boy' as she moves up the social hierarchy – except the protagonists in this familiar teen-movie plot are actually Chester Zoo's chimpanzees." The article claimed this episode reaffirmed just how similar these apes are to humans, with our shared love of drama and complicated love lives. "Chimp Boris took on the role of knight in shining armour with real enthusiasm when new female Vila was introduced to the group. Dominant male Dylan's 'hostile welcome' for Vila made for tense viewing, as keepers explained how 'tricky and dangerous' it is to bring a female into an established community. 'I can't think of anything more frightening than being chased by a whole group of chimps... Chimps give Freddy Kruger nightmares,' was hardly a ringing endorsement from veteran keeper Niall.

Canny Vila eventually learned to keep her head down and a 'swan song' blossomed between her and the older and wiser Boris.

It wasn't meant to be though, as Vila soon had her head turned by Dylan and Boris was no longer flavour of the month. But thankfully it wasn't all doom and gloom for Boris, as he celebrated reaching his 50th birthday with a cake and, ever the gentleman, even shared it with old flame Vila." [4]

ENDNOTES

1   Downloaded on 21.1.2020 from https://www.wirralglobe.co.uk/news/7419718.boris-and-

mum-are-reunited/

2	Downloaded on 22 .1.2020 from https://www.cheshire-live.co.uk/whats-on/secret-life-zoo-tv-presenter-10976890

3	Downloaded on 22.1.2020 from https://howardwilliamsblog.wordpress.com/2019/06/15/back-boris/

4	Downloaded on 22.1.2020 from https://www.cheshire-live.co.uk/news/chester-cheshire-news/secret-life-zoo-proves-just-12739253

CHAPTER 5: GEORGE MOTTERSHEAD AND HIS FAMILY

In "Our Zoo" June Mottershead describes how her earliest memory is of the night she arrived with her mother, sister, a woolly monkey, two goats and two lovebirds at Oakfield in a removal van.[1] Her father wasn't with them as he was in Derbyshire collecting two Canadian black bears which he'd been offered at a knockdown price if he could trap them. The house was completely bare, the garden overgrown and it was so cold that they spent the night together huddled together fully clothed in the same bed to keep warm.

The Mottershead family's market garden business was based in Shavington near Crewe and George Mottershead collected animals such as lizards and insects that arrived with exotic plants imported by the business. As an 8-year old boy, a visit to Belle Vue Zoo in Manchester in 1903 fuelled his developing interest in creating a zoo of his own. Instead of being thrilled by the sight of the animals in cages catching sweets and titbits thrown to them by the jeering and whistling crowds, George was shocked. He felt the animals were not being treated with the respect they deserved, and over supper that night he announced that he knew what he wanted to do when he grew up. He was going to build a zoo – a zoo without bars.

George left school at thirteen and became a "physical culture instructor", or bodybuilder. He was severely wounded in the First World War during the battle of the Somme and ended up at a hospital in Knotty Ash, Liverpool, where the family were told that he would end his days in a wheelchair. His brother Stanley died during the war, three days before his eldest daughter Muriel was born. Through sheer determination George regained the use of his legs and within three years he could walk unaided. The family moved to the smallholding in Shavington in 1919 where they grew fruit, flowers and vegetables. However, in 1926 the General Strike and start of the great depression brought the family to the brink of bankruptcy. The solution was to set up a small zoo and charge 6d entrance fee. George's collection of animals grew, and he began to search for a suitable home for his zoo. He chose Oakfield Manor, a red-brick mansion set in nine acres with orchards and a stable block in Upton by Chester, a country village a couple of miles from Chester and with easy access by railway to Chester and Birkenhead. He bought the manor for £3,500 in 1930, a knockdown price, as prior to the crash it would have been worth six times more. The bank had refused to lend him more than £2300, but he managed to persuade his father-in-law to come to the rescue with a private mortgage. There were local objections, and the local council turned down the application for planning permission for a zoo in November 1930. The local residents fired up by Rev. Toogood, the vicar of Upton, organised a petition against the zoo, fearing that a large influx of visitors would lower the tone of the area, and with it the value of their properties, but Mottershead stuck to his guns, and Chester Zoo opened to the public on 10 June 1931.[2] Amongst the conditions imposed by the Council, there was to be no advertisement sign or noticeboard which could be seen from the road, making the zoo practically invisible. The first animals were displayed in pens in the courtyard.

George Mottershead building the zoo in 1931

The zoo made national headlines in July 1932 but not for reasons anyone would have wished for. The headline "Monkey Commits Suicide" appeared all over the national newspapers. One of the macaques had chewed off a piece of rope and tied it onto a branch. On the other end of the rope he made a noose with a slipknot, put his head in the noose and jumped off the branch, breaking his neck and dying instantly.[3] Was it a deliberate suicide or just a tragic accident? Whichever it was, it helped to put the zoo on the map and people from further afield got to hear about the zoo. But financially the zoo was proving to be a disaster, with fewer visitors in the two years since it had opened than came through the gate in the last six months at Shavington. The easy solution would have been to turn the zoo into an amusement park, but this went against everything that George had fought for. The solution was to turn the zoo into a non-profit-making society, and in September 1932 the Chester Zoological Society was founded, with a hierarchy of founder members, benefactors, patrons and life members, with various privileges for each category of member. Its objective was "to encourage the humane treatment of wild animals and birds and assist in the preservation of wild animals and bird life in this country." [4] However, this still failed to raise enough money to keep the zoo afloat and in 1934 the North of England Zoological Society Limited was formed, with an elected council chaired by Richard Blair Young. Mottershead served as director-secretary, his wife, Elizabeth, as catering manager, his father, Albert, as head gardener, and his older daughter, Muriel, as assistant curator. His younger daughter, June, developed a special interest in fish, and an aquarium with six cold-water tanks was built in the basement of the Oakfield. Geraldine Russell Allen, who later chaired the zoo council, sponsored the aquarium which was opened by Lady Daresbury in 1934. The same year the monkey house was rebuilt, and a penguin pool was added. A black-footed penguin chick hatched successfully. There were not many visitors however, and the zoo relied on the support of benefactors. The Holt family, famous for running a shipping company, donated many animals, including mandrills and chimpanzees from West Africa, while the fifth Duke of Westminster presented the zoo with a capybara. [5]

In 1937 a new lion house was opened by Lord Leverhulme with African lions from Bristol and Dublin zoos. Mottershead wanted to build a large, outdoor lion enclosure surrounded by 12-foot-high chain-link fencing, rather than the thick metal bars which were normally used for cages for lions. Almost half of the council opposed this idea, worrying that the lions would escape, and many council members resigned. Mottershead later proposed an adoption scheme, in which members of the public could pay to have a card with their name posted by their "adopted" animal's enclosure. The zoo council dragged its heels on this idea until forced to do so by financial necessity when the second world war broke out in September 1939. Mottershead used to broadcast regularly on the BBC's Children's Hour and used these to promote the adoption scheme, which took off in a big way. [6]

During the war, the zoo received animals evacuated from Bristol, Paignton and other zoos. In 1941 the first elephants arrived. They were stranded when Doorley's Tropical Revue closed due to the war. Supporters of the zoo offered to help pay for their care so they would not be destroyed. The elephants, Manniken and Molly, arrived on 28 August 1941 along with their mahout, Khanadas, who had cared for them for most of their life.

By 1941 the zoo had a total of 14 lions, some acquired from other zoos and others bred in Chester. In 1942 the zoo made a profit for the first time. In 1944 two new enclosures for bears were built, using inexpensive locally obtained materials, and the polar bear enclosure was constructed using recycled wartime concrete antitank blocks and pillboxes. Catherine Jane Tomkyns-Grafton, who had originally adopted Chester's first polar bear, provided funding for their new enclosure and later bequeathed the zoo £18,000, which was a very generous sum for that time. [7]

After the war ended in 1945, the polar, brown, and black bears all moved to their new enclosures. In 1947, Mottershead finally achieved his dream of keeping the lions behind chain-link fencing. During this period the zoo continued to expand and a sea lion pool, reptile house, beaver enclosure, and a flamingo pool were all added. The new elephant house continued the tradition of using surplus concrete, antitank blocks and local sandstone as the building materials. [8]

By 1949 the zoo's grounds had expanded to cover 65 acres, and visitor numbers that year reached 320,000. The zoo chose "Always Building" as its motto, with a beaver as the zoo logo. In 1950 the society became a charity and dropped the term "limited" from its title, becoming the North of England Zoological Society. During the 1950s, parrot aviaries and houses for giraffes, zebras, and camels were built. The present aquarium, built by Fred and June (Mottershead) Williams over two years in their free time , and now one of the oldest animal houses still in use at the zoo, was opened in 1952 and included a flooded flat roof with glass panels set in its base which allowed visitors to view fish from below. This was a precursor to the tunnel tanks now common in aquariums. However, the roof tank didn't work as local birds began to catch the fish and drop them around the zoo.

Two cafeterias and a souvenir shop were opened to cater for visitors' needs. During the 1950s the zoo developed extensive gardens and lawns that proved popular as picnic areas for the increasing numbers of visitors. The zoo's greenhouses during this time developed a collection of tropical plants, shrubs, and trees for use inside the new, more spacious, and better-illuminated animal buildings. [9]

Mottershead received the OBE, an honorary degree of MSc, and served as President of the International Union of Zoo Directors.

He was influenced by the ideas of Carl Hagenbeck,

who invented the modern zoo concept and by Heini Hediger, a pioneer of ethology. Mottershead took Hagenbeck's idea for moats and ditches as an alternative to cage bars, and extended their use throughout the zoo, often with species that Hagenbeck had not considered. For example, when chimpanzees were released into their new enclosure at Chester in 1956, a group of grassy islands, they were separated from visitors by no more than a 12-foot (3.7 m) water-filled moat. Nobody knew at the time if chimps could swim. It turned out that they could not, and today the chimp islands are a centrepiece of Chester Zoo. The building of a nocturnal house and quarantine premises in Birkenhead near the port of Liverpool in 1957 allowed the zoo to directly import stock from Africa, including kudu, lechwe, eland, and warthog. Large paddocks were constructed by combining the Carl Hagenbeck model bounded by ha-has (sloping ditches) with the Chester hallmarks of a surrounding low sandstone wall and flower beds. A canal system with waterbuses became a new visitor attraction at the end of the 1950s.

The present elephant house was built in 1961 as the pachyderm house; at the time it also housed rhinos, tapirs, and hippopotamuses. The zoo completed the rhinoceros and monkey houses in 1963. During this decade new motorways facilitated travel to the zoo and annual visitor figures topped 1 million for the first time.

The Tropical House (now Tropical Realm) opened on the society's 30th anniversary in 1964. Considered ahead of its time, the building included a nocturnal exhibit, indoor quarters for gorillas and pygmy hippopotamuses, as well as a reptile area. The main part of the facility, planted as a tropical forest, housed a large variety of smaller free-flying birds, with other species held in aviaries.

1968 saw the zoo closed for 11 weeks till it was cleared of having any foot and mouth disease.

In the 1970s Chester welcomed the first elephant to be born in captivity. He was named Jubilee by viewers of TV show Blue Peter. He lived at the zoo till 1998 when he was transferred to Belfast Zoo.

In 1981 an appeal for a penguin enclosure was held. It was highly successful and the new pool with underwater viewing was soon open. 12 Humboldt penguins were donated by Whipsnade Zoo with a further 12 black footed penguins moved from Amsterdam. Despite continuing improvements and expansion, following Mottershead's death in 1984, the zoo's visitor attendance reached a low of 700,000 in 1985, coinciding with a major international garden festival in Liverpool. A rift between the director and the zoo council culminated in an extraordinary meeting of zoo members in 1985. The entire council resigned, with only one re-elected at the following annual general meeting. [10]

In 1986 the zoo was surrounded by a fence to meet the standards of the Zoo Licensing Act 1981.

In 1987 the sixth Duke of Westminster became the society's first president. In 1989 Diana, Princess of Wales, opened a new chimpanzee quarters with an attractive, conical-roofed, circular "oast house" design, and in 1991 the duchess of Kent opened the zoo monorail. New standards set elsewhere for the exhibition and welfare of large mammals, together with the zoo's insufficient capital for new and expensive large-mammal developments, resulted in Chester stopping its exhibition of both gorillas and bears. This decision enabled the zoo to focus on developing large aviaries using relatively inexpensive construction methods based on the use of lightweight nylon mesh. In 1994, in keeping with the zoo's conservation efforts, endangered Asiatic lions replaced the African lions. A new public parking area and an entrance complex and shop opened in spring 1995 on the north-west side of the zoo. Perhaps the most notable of the zoo's developments in the late 1990s was the walk-through Twilight Zone bat experience. By the end of 1997 the zoo had more than 6,500 individual animals representing some 500 species and it ended the 20th century on a high note when it was named Britain's Zoo of the Year in both 1998 and 1999. [11]

In 2007 the zoo welcomed its largest number of visitors ever, when 1.3 million people visited the zoo.

During January 2009 the Natural Vision master plan was revealed. It was a £225 million vision that would see the zoo become Europe's largest conservation attraction. The first phase was to be a 56 hectare (140-acre) African rainforest-themed sanctuary. It would house chimps, gorillas, okapi, tropical birds and other species. It was also to have a hotel, conservation college and revamped entrance connecting to a marina that was to be built on zoo land. During 2011 these plans were shelved when £40 million potential funding was lost when the North West Regional Development Agency was abolished. In 2011 the zoo created Act for Wildlife a separate brand and identity for their conservation projects. 2012 saw the opening of the first underwater viewing zone for giant otters in the UK. This cutting-edge habitat was opened by the Lord Mayor. The Natural Vision plan was subsequently modified – the Islands were completed in 2015 and currently there are new plans for a hotel complex overlooking a safari grasslands park.

ENDNOTES

1   Mottershead, J. 2014. Our Zoo. London, Headline, pp 1-50

2   Downloaded on 22.1.2020 from https://en.wikipedia.org/wiki/Chester_Zoo#History

3   Mottershead (2014) ibid, p78

4   ibid, p81

5   Downloaded on 10.2.2020 from http://www.historyofuptonbychester.org.uk/zoo.html

6-11   ibid

CHAPTER 6 OUR ZOO – THE DRAMA

In 2014 the BBC broadcast a six-part mini-series called Our Zoo", starring Lee Ingelby, Liz White and Anne Reid. The storyline closely followed the real-life history of the zoo as recounted by June Mottershead in "Our Zoo".

The plot of each episode is summarized on the IMDB website: [1]

In episode 1, George Mottershead, still tormented by memories of the Great War, where his brother died, is collecting supplies from Liverpool docks for his father Albert's shop when he sees an abandoned monkey and parrot, which he brings home. He plans to sell Mortimer, the monkey, to a circus but instead ends up rescuing an elderly camel. Younger daughter June is thrilled by the menagerie in the backyard, other family members less so. Then George accidentally comes across the dilapidated Oakfield Manor in the village of Upton, which is up for auction. Encouraged by friendly aristocrat Lady Katherine Longmore George secures a bank loan and, assisted by

Albert, who sells his shop, buys the manor with a view to turning it into a zoo without bars. The family moves into the manor but, despite support from his wife Lizzie, George's sour mother Lucy and elder daughter Muriel, are not impressed and matters are not helped when Mortimer escapes and creates havoc in the village store.

In Episode 2, George receives more animals for his zoo as well as rescuing a fox from a hunt led by vicar Aaron Webb. Muriel is befriended by Lady Katherine whilst Lucy is still negative about the move. Lizzie goes to the council to get a business licence and is overwhelmed by the paperwork involved but finally triumphs to George's delight. George himself rescues two bears from a cave in Matlock and, helped by brother-in-law Billy, brings them to the zoo. One of the bears is sick but the village doctor sees her and appears to be an ally. Webb on the other hand, whilst charming Lizzie, is leading the villagers' opposition to the zoo, getting information from the unsuspecting June to present to the council.

In Episode 3, whilst the family nurses Eve the bear back to full health, Webb and shopkeeper Camilla Radler hold a community meeting with the intention of getting the zoo closed. George sees this as an opportunity to win over the opposition by pitching his vision of the zoo to them, but he is shouted down. He is, however, cheered when a journalist named Gascoigne from the "Chester Herald" comes to write an article on the zoo; but this too fails, as the visit is less than successful, and the finished piece portrays George as inept and unrealistic. On the positive side Muriel, previously opposed to her father's plans, becomes more sympathetic as she sees how much the project means to him; and Billy brings in a batch of new arrivals to charm the enemy - a dozen penguins.

In Episode 4, Adam, the male bear, escapes and although George and Billy manage to retrieve him before he reaches the village, George is injured in June's sight and confined to bed. He knows he must finish the bears' enclosure, but the bank will not supply any more funds. Fortunately, he meets Lady Katherine's friend Lady Goodwin, an eccentric aristocrat who supports him and who stages a glamorous benefit evening at Selbourne Hall, hosted by Lady Katherine and to which Camilla Radler's postman son Archie escorts Muriel. The evening goes well until one of the guests accuses Katherine of being an adulteress. Furthermore, Mrs. Radler and the duplicitous Webb are gathering signatures to close the zoo, leading to planning permission being denied and a confrontation between Webb and George.

In Episode 5, Frankie, a council secretary dating Billy, shows George that Camilla Radler lied in order to get her petition signed to stop the zoo and he confronts her but, even with the money from the fund raising event, finances are at an all-time low and George has to sell Adam to Belle Vue zoo on the promise of retrieving him in better days. Following her disgrace Katherine is hiding away but on discovering that her nephew Aldous works for Sir Arthur Addison, the deputy minister of health, who approves planning permission appeals, George persuades her to go to London with him where they button-hole Sir Arthur, resulting in permission for a public hearing. Back at the zoo Muriel's efforts to get work as a typist, helped by Archie, whom she encourages to stand up to his mother, are more successful than June's idea to give the villagers camel rides whilst Eve gives birth to two cubs.

In the final episode, the hearing to determine whether the zoo may operate results in some surprises but does not settle the matter. The next day, the judge and public tour the zoo. Eventually, the verdict arrives in the post.

The series received some very positive reviews, e.g. "This is an inspiring story with all the elements needed in a drama to keep the viewer entertained. The acting is superb in it and the sets and costumes take you back to the wonderful era of the 1930s." [2]

But other reviewers were quite critical, e.g. "George might be an idealist and you do find yourself rooting for him, but there is something rather derivative about Our Zoo. Maybe it wants to channel the success of Call the Midwife but got nowhere near reaching the levels of All Creatures Great and Small and is not helped by its grim colours and gloomy mood. A drama about a zoo should have been bright and colourful. The show never quite took off in the ratings and ended up being cancelled after one series by the BBC." [3]

"Cheshire Live" announcing the demise of the show reported, "Our Zoo, the popular and well received TV drama about the history of Chester Zoo will not return for a second series, the BBC has confirmed." Despite pulling in more than 5 million viewers per episode during its six-part run earlier in 2014, and being nominated for two National TV Awards, Our Zoo had not been renewed for another series. The writer felt that this news would come as a huge disappointment to fans of the show, many of whom described it as "the best thing on TV in ages." [4]

But a BBC spokesperson told The Chronicle that although it was 'very proud' of the show, a 'hard choice' had to be made.

"We are very proud of Our Zoo and would like to thank all those involved," the spokesperson said. "However, in order to create room for new shows and to keep increasing the range of BBC One drama we sometimes have to make hard choices and it will not be returning for a second series."

The Zoo's Head of Marketing, Caroline Sanger-Davies, was reported to have said that the tourist attraction had experienced a huge surge of popularity during the show's primetime run. "It's definitely made a big impression," she said at the time. "We've gathered postcodes from visitors this September compared to last September and they have really shown a spread of people travelling here from various places. September is very well supported usually but we have definitely seen visitors from further afield which we attribute to the success of Our Zoo." [5]

A petition requesting the BBC to produce a second series got more than a thousand signatures but to no avail.

ENDNOTES

1   Downloaded on 31.1.2020 from https://www.imdb.com/title/tt3620824/episodes?season=1&ref_=tt_eps_sn_1

2   Downloaded on 31.1.2020 from https://www.imdb.com/review/rw3094437/?ref_=tt_urv

3   Downloaded on 31.1.2020 from https://www.imdb.com/review/rw3141611/?ref_=tt_urv

4   Downloaded on 31.1.2020 from https://www.cheshire-live.co.uk/news/chester-cheshire-news/bbc-confirms-no-second-series-8260107

CHAPTER 7 BREAK-INS AND BREAK-OUTS

There appears to be a small group of crazies who delight in breaking into zoos and other attractions under cover of darkness, filming their exploits and posting the vlogs on YouTube and other social media. Ally Law's exploits include breaking into London Zoo. [1]

According to Wikipedia, Law started his YouTube channel in December 2014. The first video he uploaded was of him performing parkour on the top of buildings in Southampton city centre, filmed on a GoPro camera. Law has climbed in multiple locations around the world, such as Melbourne, Dubai, Bangkok, and Barcelona.

After trespassing in Thorpe Park to climb the Stealth roller coaster in July 2017, and breaking into the Celebrity Big Brother house twice in January 2018, Law was given a 5 year criminal behaviour order that bans him from areas of any bridges or buildings not open to the public, any business property outside business hours, and was given a lifetime ban at all properties owned by Merlin Entertainment.

Law also does 'overnight challenges', where he and a group of friends will attempt to stay in a range of commercial premises after closing hours.

Law's YouTube channel passed one million subscribers in May 2018, passing the two million subscriber mark on 14 October 2018. In May 2018 he tweeted, "One million people? Fucking unbelievable! Massive thanks to every single one of you that support me every single day. I've dreamt of this moment ever since I created my channel 3 1/2 years ago! The journey has been a madness but just know, this is just the beginning." [2]

He also passed the 3 million subscriber mark in December 2019, despite a 5-month long absence from YouTube due to legal reasons.

In October 2017 Cheshire Live reported under the headline "Thrill-seeking YouTubers who broke into Chester Zoo slammed for 'extremely dangerous' stunt" that a group of six youths had broken into the zoo at dead of night. [3] It's not clear if these were Ally Law and his friends, although it seems very likely.

The zoo had condemned the group's 'unacceptable' behaviour which left a zebra injured and was reported to be taking legal action against vloggers who filmed themselves breaking in and startling an endangered species of zebra causing an injury.

At one stage the 'overnight challenge' video, posted on YouTube, reveals three of the thrill-seekers climbing over a fence into an animal enclosure in the dark. Moments later the young men, who were carrying torches, run away believing they have disturbed a rhino. It appears the group, numbering about half a dozen, was spotted by a security guard who gave chase, but they got away.

Zoo chief operating officer Jamie Christon condemned the actions of the video bloggers, or vloggers, saying they showed no regard for their own safety or that of the animals. He was quoted as saying, [4]

"We're aware of the small group who trespassed onto the zoo site a couple of weeks ago and we are taking legal action. There was damage to zoo property including a set of customer toilets following the trespass. It appears that the group also startled a Grevy's zebra, an endangered species who we care for as part of a Europe wide breeding programme, as the animal had an injury to its hind leg following the trespass. Thankfully the animal has since been making a good recovery, helped by our senior keepers and veterinary teams who were quickly on site. With over 15,000 animals in our care, including large carnivores and predators, trespass onto the site is both unacceptable and extremely dangerous. The members of the group appear to have little or no regard for their own safety, or the safety and welfare of the animals. We condemn the irresponsible actions of the group and are taking the matter extremely seriously."

The video posted on YouTube is one of a series showing dangerous stunts. It begins with two young men on the roof of a high rise building in Manchester city centre. Then the action switches to a swimming pool where an individual from the male-only group disrupts a tournament by jumping from the top of a 10m diving board as people swim below – potentially endangering the swimmers and apparently hurting his own knees in the fall. That evening the group are shown heading by car to Chester Zoo, where the gang meet up in the dark before scaling a high gate. Signs for the animal enclosures can be seen by torchlight such as the 'Monkeys entrance', black rhinos and meerkats.

Cheshire Live reports that at one point a couple of the vloggers climb over a fence into an enclosure and gingerly approach an animal in the darkness before making a hasty retreat thinking it is a rhino, although in fact it was a zebra. The video picks up signs for the chimpanzee house and the animals can be heard in the background. A giraffe's head can also be seen in the torchlight.

The vloggers decide to scarper as the animals are making so much noise, and they feel sure it will attract the attention of on-site security. Safely back at home, the narrator concludes: "The whole vlog was a madness, broken knees and breaking into the zoo, what more could you want?" [5]

Comments from Liverpool Echo readers included, "Mindless morons, a clue for you next time you do something this stupid, the rhino is grey, very big and has a large horn (or sometimes two horns), on its nose. Zebras are smaller, striped black and white and don't have horns. Next time you fancy a challenge could I suggest you try the lion enclosure; they will be easy to identify; they will be the animals tearing one of you to pieces." (from

Hobgoblin) and "It's a reflection of how "intelligent" these morons were that they could mistake a zebra for a rhino. I mean they are virtually identical aren't they!" (from Red Squirrel). [6]

According to The Standard, the footage was subsequently deleted from YouTube. [7]

As well as humans trying to break into the zoo, there have been various instances of animals trying to break out. The Independent noted in 2019 that dozens of British zoos had been warned by inspectors for failing to carry out adequate emergency drills for dealing with escaped animals.

According to one of over 150 inspection reports country-wide from 2016 to 2018, a tentacled snake exhibit at Chester was found unpadlocked, with inspectors concluding it could be opened by a member of the public. The zoo told The Independent that the lock was out of sight and it was "extremely unlikely" a visitor could reach it – but that a secure lock had since been added. [8]

In 2009 Cheshire Live reported on a number of animal escapes from the zoo over the years. A curious orangutan climbed out of its cage in 2003, forcing hundreds of visitors to take refuge in the restaurant, tropical house and cafes. It spent about 90 minutes sitting on the roof of the enclosure but later lowered itself back into the cage and went to sleep. An investigation revealed the animal had, over several days, lifted and removed roofing tiles to the enclosure, which housed five other orang-utans.

Back in 1996 an escaped chimpanzee was shot dead as

it attacked a keeper. After an anaesthetic dart failed to knock out the 30-year-old ape, another keeper fired the fatal shot that killed the chimpanzee.

A bull elephant went berserk after escaping the confines of the elephant enclosure and smashing through the zoo's perimeter fence 26 years ago. The animal got as far as Caughall Road, a mile away from the Zoo, before it was shot dead. [9]

In July 2009 the Daily Mail reported there was panic amongst 5000 visitors to the zoo as 30 chimpanzees managed to escape from their enclosure. [10] The escape led to panic as zoo staff first hid visitors in nearby buildings, before deciding to escort them out of the zoo premises as a security measure. The animals had managed to slip out of the back of their outdoor enclosure into a much less secure keepers' area. The keepers feared the chimpanzees would escape and run wild among the crowds. However, the crafty chimps instead tucked into their food, kept in the keepers' kitchen in advance of lunch, and they were still a locked door away from the public.

The zoo website quotes George Mottershead describing how Sammy, a large Malayan bear, managed to escape:

"We do not like the excitement caused by escaped animals, firstly because they disorganise everything, and secondly they do not inspire confidence among the nervous section of the public, but they have happened and will happen even in the best regulated zoo. It was on Saturday November 27th that we had such excitement, breakfast had just been completed and the staff had returned to their work, when Rob-Rob the blue and red macaw who spends most of his time on a stand in the kitchen [in Oakfield], gave a yell which had long since become a warning that something out of the ordinary is taking place. At once those in the kitchen looked up to see the cause and were horrified to see Sammy the large Malayan Bear walking round the top of the kitchen garden wall. The alarm was at once given and the staff mobilised, in the meantime Sammy had descended into the kitchen garden so it was decided to keep him there if possible while a means of catching him was thought out, so each side of the wall was patrolled and whenever he tried to mount it he was driven down. Once he gained mastery and walked along the top of the polar bear den, but fortunately was driven back. It was decided, if possible, to drive him into the Potting Shed and Fruit Store, and then endeavour to get him to enter a travelling crate. Fortunately, after about an hour we succeeded in doing this, and he was taken back to his home. Sammy was put back in his home, but before leaving him the cause of his escape was rectified." [11]

In January 2018 the satirical website Chester Bugle reported that an entire family of Meerkats had managed to escape from their enclosure. "The meerkats formed a ladder by standing on each other's shoulders, before they were able to reach the top, and the escapees climbed the ladder to exit over the top wall. The meerkats who formed the ladder were left behind by the escaping family. As many as seven meerkats are believed to have escaped. The meerkats were last spotted in Ewloe, outside the Moneysupermarket.com offices.

A spokesperson for Chester Zoo commented:
'Please do not approach the meerkats. They may seem cute and friendly but they're hostile to humans and they protect their pack. Any attempt to approach them, or handle them, could be met with extreme aggression.'

It isn't known why the meerkats chose today to escape, or why they have headed to Ewloe and towards the Moneysupermarket.com offices." [12]

And on Twitter... "Someone thought a leopard had escaped from Chester zoo. Turned out one of the moms from the local primary school lost their dressing gown on the school run..." [13]

In 2017 four orangutans escaped while the Duke of Westminster was visiting the zoo. Two female Sumatran orangutans, Subis and Indah and two of Subis's young offspring made their way out of their enclosed area just after 10am. A zoo spokesperson confirmed that they stayed safely within the zoo's Monsoon Forest building while primate keepers quickly ushered them back into their enclosure. No visitors were in the vicinity at the time as the building was closed for a private event due to start later in the day, the spokesperson said. He added: "The Duke of Westminster was here today but obviously not involved in the incident." Mike Jordan, the zoo's collections director, said: "Subis, Tuti, Siska and Indah were spotted by one of our primate keepers and the team were quickly on hand. Orangutans are extremely curious animals and were being rascals about returning but they're all now back safe and sound. No visitors were in the immediate area but, just to be on the safe side, an area was cordoned off by our emergency response team for a short while until we were sure the family and Indah were back safely with the rest of the group. We'd like to thank those visitors for their patience." [14]

ENDNOTES

1   Downloaded on 31.1.2020 from https://www.youtube.com/watch?v=M8CkbDQHk4U

2   Downloaded on 31.1.2020 from https://twitter.com/allyalaw/status/994298759113830400?lang=en-gb

3   Downloaded on 31.1.2020 from https://www.cheshire-live.co.uk/news/chester-cheshire-news/thrill-seeking-youtubers-who-broke-13838911

4   ibid

5   ibid

6   Downloaded on 31.1.2020 from https://www.liverpoolecho.co.uk/news/liverpool-news/youtube-pranksters-flee-lives-after-13842753

7   Downloaded on 31.1.2020 from https://www.chesterstandard.co.uk/news/15965007.chester-zoo-condemns-overnight-break-in-by-youtube-bloggers/

8   Downloaded on 31.1.2020 from
https://inews.co.uk/news/uk/zoo-safety-concerns-animal-
parks-warned-inspectors-failing-emergency-drills-
112665

9   Downloaded on 31.1.2020 from
https://www.cheshire-live.co.uk/news/chester-cheshire-
news/more-great-escapes-chester-zoo-5219702

10   Downloaded on 31.1.2020 from
https://www.dailymail.co.uk/news/article-
1197741/Panic-5-000-visitors-Chester-Zoo-30-
chimpanzees-escape-enclosure.html

11   Downloaded on 31.1.2020 from
https://www.chesterzoo.org/memories/bear-escapes/

12   Downloaded on 31.1.2020 from
https://www.chesterbugle.co.uk/2018/01/16/family-
meerkats-escapes-chester-zoo/

13   Downloaded on 31.1.2020 from
https://www.thepoke.co.uk/2020/01/29/escaped-leopard-
false-alarm/

14   Downloaded on 31.1.2020 from
https://www.cheshire-live.co.uk/news/chester-cheshire-
news/four-orangutans-escape-chester-zoo-11535966

15   Downloaded on 31.1.2020 from
https://www.dailymail.co.uk/news/article-
4128824/Orangutan-ESCAPES-enclosure-Chester-
Zoo.html

CHAPTER 8 LANTERNS, BUGS AND PREDATORS.

As well as animal collections, many zoos put on displays or events which are animal-related but do not actually feature live animals. These bring in additional revenue for the zoo and allow for any surpluses to be used to further the zoo's purpose – which in the case of Chester Zoo is "preventing extinction".

Since 2012, Chester has organised an annual "Lanterns" event in the run-up to Christmas. The Lantern Company was commissioned by the zoo to organise the first event and announced in November 2012:

"The Lantern Company have been working round the clock to create a life size animal lantern menagerie and glowing costumed characters for Chester Zoo's Lantern Magic event. Bring your family and friends for an unforgettably magical journey through the wonderful gardens of the zoo this winter and get up close to our toweringly tall giraffe, amazing Asian elephant, Sumatran tiger and many more favourite animals in this wonderfully real lantern display." [1] Previews were held on November

24th and 25th and then the event ran every weekend until December 23rd, 2012.

The Lantern Company was well qualified to take on this event. Their website announced, "The work we make (sic) ranges from small scale theatrical experiences to spectacular outdoor shows, from community arts workshops to specialist training, from giant puppets and kinetic processional floats to beautiful sculptural lanterns. We create work for both day and night-time events." [2]

The first Lanterns event attracted generally glowing praise. One reviewer commented, "What a magical evening full of lamps, lights and of course lantern. The children had sooo much fun. The evening was well organised and flowed well, full of little surprises, mini hot chocolates and elves that light up! Santa was a bit of a disappointment, but the glowing animals were amazing. Food was delicious too. Also the adults had fun too especially if you take in the beauty of the lights at night." [(3)]

Overall the event was judged a success, and the zoo repeated it the following year, when Cheshire Live reported, "The first evening of the event prompted a great reaction on social media with one person on Twitter labelling it 'enchanting and magical' and another taking to Facebook to say it had left the family with the 'happiest memories'." [(4)] The zoo responded to popular demand by making a limited number of extra tickets available for each night of the event between Thursday 19 December and Monday 23 December.

By now the Lanterns was becoming an annual event, and in 2014 there were again many positive reviews. One reviewer wrote, "Decided to visit Chester Zoo's Lantern Magic this year. It was really worth a trip, the twinkling lights in the trees and colourful lanterns lit your way around the zoo, there was a magical atmosphere. Father Christmas, Elves and Mrs Claus were around to show you the way to a beautiful display of lit up life-size models of the animals. Especially impressive was the giant Owl which was very effective. Everyone was really friendly and welcoming. Father Christmas was waiting at the end of the walk and a professional photograph with him was only £4, albeit you could take your own pictures, if you wished. A Magical Evening." [5]

In 2015 the zoo made some changes to the previously tried and tested format. Cheshire Live reported,

'Inspired by the larger-than-life animal lanterns children will also have the opportunity to get creative and make their very own version to take home. Managing director Jamie Christon said: "Lantern Magic is a magical, after hours experience that lets visitors explore the zoo after dark. Friends and families will use their very own glowing lanterns to light the way through our beautiful gardens and past our larger-than-life animal illuminations. There'll also be the chance to catch a glimpse of Santa as he drives through the zoo on his sleigh. This event has been a magnificent addition to the zoo in previous years and, being bigger and better than ever before this time around, it's sure to deliver a heart-warming experience for all of the family." [6]

The Lantern Company announced, "Over the last 3 years, we have been commissioned by Chester Zoo to create a spectacular display of life size animal lanterns for the festive night-time event, Lantern Magic.

This year is the most ambitious event to date – we are creating a whole host of new animal lanterns, and dozens of illuminated animal puppets and enchanting characters for visitors of all ages to discover, as they take a lantern lit stroll round the zoo at night. And don't miss the glowing tropical gardens, the giant butterfly lantern lawns, condor's nest or the pedal powered crazy snowflake contraptions, to mention but a few of the wonderful sights you can expect to see!" [7]

In 2016 the zoo continued to follow the previous formula, with the Liverpool Echo announcing, "These Chester Zoo Christmas lanterns will make your eyes light up! The Lanterns at Chester Zoo feature wild animals and creatures native to the UK. Families can marvel over the illuminated life-sized animals as they journey around the zoo with their own cloth lantern for the grown-ups and little cup lanterns for the kids including a flickering LED tealight. The little ones can also enjoy interactive performances from live puppet lantern characters including ostriches, flamingos and even a spider. But no Christmas event would be complete without a visit for the big man himself. As you follow the path, you will meet Santa's elves before glimpsing Father Christmas on his lit-up sleigh - with a special treat of a satsuma or biscuit - but only if you've been good! [8]

The following year the zoo made some fairly drastic changes to the earlier tried and tested formula. 'Ultimate', a Manchester-based creative design agency was commissioned to drive these changes forward and 'Wild Rumpus' provided actors dressed as animals who interacted with the public.

Ultimate defended its brief as follows, "Winter is traditionally a quiet period for zoos, but at Chester The

Lanterns has dramatically changed that. Each year thousands of people brave the cold to experience a touch of festive magic. After all, when else do you have the chance to visit the zoo after dark? Our brief was to attract more people than ever before, whilst still appealing to the previous visitors who loved it so much.

Sunset over Madagascar Play

In 2017, The Lanterns event was slightly different from previous years as it became a more theatrical experience. In addition to the magnificent lanterns themselves, there were also outstanding performances by aerial acrobats, musicians and roller skaters. As part of this change, there was a stronger storyline throughout The Lanterns journey for the audience to engage with and follow as they walked around. At first, they thought that the journey was simple, with presents piled high and the postal workers rushing to answer all of the letters to Santa, making sure that every child got just what they wished for. Then they saw that this magical world is full of real animals from all over the world. Animals that inspire us to stop, to look and to wonder what they would wish for Christmas. Because there is a little bit of magic in every animal at the zoo. The lantern route was filled to the brim with sacks of lantern toys, boxes of lantern presents, and huge post boxes for children and families to post their own letters. Our creative campaign needed to reflect the wonder, magic and excitement created by each animal character.

Whatever direction we chose to take with the creative campaign, it was crucial that it still remained recognisably Chester Zoo. We needed to link The Lanterns story with the Chester Zoo brand values, inspiring people about the natural world and engendering a spirit of playfulness." [9]

Cheshire Live reported, "The annual family Christmas spectacle which sees the zoo transformed into an enchanting world of animal-inspired adventure, has become a much loved occasion on the festive calendar, growing more in popularity over the last five years. Ticket demand is always high, and that's also been the case for the 2017 event which officially opened last Friday (November 24), with much anticipation for the new features that include a theatrical trail through the zoo, created with outdoor arts producers Wild Rumpus.

2017 was the first year I was involved with Lanterns at the zoo. Most evenings I was standing by a barrier directing the crowd, stopping people walking off the route

into the dark. I collected a repertoire of jokes to keep people amused when the queue to see Santa perched ten feet up in the air hadn't moved for several minutes! One of my favourites was, "Why did the lion cross the road? To get to the other pride!"

Caterpillars near the zoo entrance

Small children were given a decorated tin bucket with a battery operated candle, which they could take home with them. The adults, on the other hand, had a triangular cloth pyramid on the end of a pole, with a battery operated light mounted inside. Because of the huge numbers of visitors, these were limited to one lantern per group, but even this didn't stop many people from abandoning their lanterns half-way round the route. One of our tasks was to go around the route collecting abandoned lanterns and carrying them on our shoulders or in a tilt truck back to the entrance so they could be given out to other groups. It was interesting to observe that where very few lanterns had been abandoned, people carried on with them, but when several were abandoned in the same place, the "lemming" principle seemed to come into effect, and lots of other people abandoned theirs also.

The zoo listened to feedback from the public and made some changes to the Lanterns the following year. Cheshire Live's reporter Carmella de Lucia commented,[10] "It feels somewhat bizarre to go to Chester Zoo and not actually see any real animals. But seeing the spectacular life sized animal illuminations at the annual Lanterns Parade gives you the chance to see the zoo as you've never seen it before - and it really is every bit as magical as it sounds. Although I'm a regular visitor to the zoo I'd never actually been to the Lanterns Parade before, but with a two-year-old daughter who is just becoming aware of Christmas, it was imperative we got to experience for ourselves this winter spectacular I'd heard so much about.

They have teamed up with Wild Rumpus to produce this year's parade which features a brand new route, new animals including sun bears, cheetahs and mandrills (as well as some of the old ones), and nine amazing spaces to explore, each with a different theme and different animals. When we arrived, my little one was given her own mini lantern (safely lit with an LED tealight) which she clutched onto fiercely throughout the entire route, and we adults were invited to pick our own much bigger lantern to carry.

We had chosen the 4.00 p.m. parade (they run every 20 minutes) so it was just turning dark when we entered the 'Garden of Delight' space which was surrounded with 10ft illuminated flowers, then onto 'Moonlit Meadow' where we saw giraffes, zebras, lions and rhinos, all of whom kindly allowed us to give them a pet on the nose. It really was like being in another world; you genuinely feel like you're in some kind of festive animal universe a million miles away from Chester.

Each space seems even more impressive than the last, from seeing Santa and his reindeer in the Northern Lights space to the Enchanted Woodland which features an amazing wall of twinkling lights. For us, it was the penguins in the Ice Kingdom who really stole the show. I have truly never heard my daughter giggle as much as when the penguin 'regurgitated' the fish she placed into his mouth.

🐾 🎄 ◻ One more sleep until it's officially Christmas at the zoo! ❄ 🎅 🎄

Here's a sneak peek at this year's Great Expedition at The Lanterns 🦋 🦍 ☠ 🐘

Along the way we were given 3D glasses that made the lights change colour when you looked at them and staff were giving out biscuits to the children too. There's also a Christmas market where you can get all manner of festive food (I wimped out of trying a Christmas burrito) and a snow machine outside the recently renovated Oakfield House, which looked incredible festooned with its Christmas splendour.

About halfway through the route, which lasts just over an hour, I took a look around and every child's face I saw was just in complete awe of the magic on display at the Chester Zoo's Lanterns Parade. To be honest, I was in awe myself. And that's all you can ask for really isn't it?"

Back in July 2013 the BBC's Newsround reported that a giant tarantula that was 33 FEET wide had joined Chester Zoo - but went on to say, "Don't worry, it's a robot!" The BBC reported, "It's one of 13 larger-than-life animatronic bugs in a new exhibition that lets visitors get extremely up close to creepy crawlies. As well as spiders, there is a praying mantis and emperor scorpion! The bug robots have been created by Billings Productions in the USA." Travis Reid said: "There's a lot of research involved. First, we would bring in specimens and study those. Then we'd actually take a 3D scanner and then we'd blow them up from there. Then we'd go back and add clay for all the details." [11]

According to Cheshire Live, the huge creations were custom-built for the zoo by a top animation studio in Texas and it was the first time they had ever been seen all together, anywhere in the world. Conservationists from the zoo hoped the exhibition would provide a showcase for invertebrates and the need to conserve threatened species.

The Zoo's director general, Mark Pilgrim, said: "Chester Zoo is heavily involved in vital world-wide conservation work aimed at saving species from extinction.

And it's not just iconic species such as Eastern black rhino and Asian elephants that we're focused on. Our work with invertebrates, like our critically endangered Polynesian tree snails or rare British fen-raft spiders, is just as important to us. We want Bugs! to put invertebrates in the spotlight, show how fantastic they are and really raise awareness of the need to conserve them. Engaging people, particularly youngsters, with conservation sometimes takes some drastic ideas and new ways of thinking and that's precisely what we hope these 13 giant robotic bugs will do. [12]

"Predators" was an exhibition of huge animatronic creations which the zoo staged in 2019. The Zoo website announced in May 2019, "Thirteen life-sized animatronic hunters – built in America – are set to star in the new show, titled Predators, which opens at the zoo this Saturday!

The never-before-seen exhibition is set to showcase over 200 million years of lost species. Featuring realistic movements and sounds, the models will include the infamous T-Rex – the most feared land predator of all time – a shark which had a bite that was three metres wide and a giant snake that ate crocodiles for breakfast. Zoo conservationists hope the high-tech creatures will highlight that extinction is a very real threat to animals on the planet today. Phil Blackburn, Zoo Ranger, said: "This collection of robotic predators is a super-sized new exhibition that has never before been seen, anywhere in the world. It's amazing to see the sheer size and scale of some of the mega beasts that once walked the planet but it's also a real reminder about the threat of extinction many species face today. It's heart-breaking to think that, one day, future generations may only be able to see animatronic jaguars, tigers and lions because they too have been wiped out. That's what we want to highlight with this new display – and that it's vital we act now to prevent the extinction of species while we still have the chance." [13]

Visitors got to see these creatures:

Megalodon: an extinct species which was longer than a humpback whale. It last swam the oceans 2.6 million years ago.

Titanoboa: The largest snake ever discovered, this vast carnivore would hunt in a similar way to modern day constrictors but could eat crocodiles and large mammals!

Giant terror bird: This 3m-high bird couldn't fly, but its strong legs and sharp beak made it a ferocious hunter – even eating small horses.

Sea scorpion: One of the biggest arthropods ever, the 8-foot-long sea scorpion would eat aquatic creatures and may have even been cannibalistic.

Smilodon: This sabre-toothed big cat could open its mouth to 120 degrees and use its enormous teeth to bring down bison across the Americas.

Megalania: A seriously oversized relative of the Komodo dragon, this Australian lizard may have been the biggest venomous creature in history.

Giant bear: Native to South America, this ancient relative of the Andean bear is the biggest bear that ever lived. Its size and strength meant it could even steal food from a ferocious sabre-toothed cat.

Dire wolf: Given celebrity status by TV series Game of Thrones, dire wolves were pack hunters who worked together to bring down prey.

Allosaurus: With sharp claws and powerful teeth, these 4-tonne dinosaurs thrived across the planet in the Jurassic period.

Dilophosaurus: This dinosaur's name means 'double-crested lizard', and famously squirted venom in the film Jurassic Park.

Sarcosuchus: Roughly the length of a double-decker bus, this giant crocodilian roamed Africa in the Cretaceous

period. It was so large it might have preyed on dinosaurs.
Utahraptor: While holding prey in its mouth, this dinosaur
would use killing claws on its feet to slash its prey.

Tyrannosaurus: Probably the most famous extinct species in history, the T-Rex is believed to have had an incredible bite strength of four metric tons. [14]

A contributor to the "Zoo Chat" discussion group asserted, "It remains a hot topic for debate whether Zoos should continue to exhibit animatronic animals alongside the real thing. In 1994 London Zoo mounted an exhibition called "Extinction". Alongside the usual suspect model T-Rex and Velociraptor, there was also a stuffed Falkland Islands Wolf, plus a range of animatronic extinct mammals of varying plausibility. The Glyptodon was dubbed by a volunteer friend of mine the mock turtle, the ground sloth bore a disconcerting resemblance to the Head Keeper of the Clore Pavilion, and at least one of the mammoths creaked audibly. However, the least convincing by some margin was an alleged Smilodon. Of this a caustic and expert carnivore manager was heard to comment "If that's what they were like, I'm not surprised they became extinct."[15]

Another contributor to "Zoo Chat" in 2017 remarked, "Chester has had temporary animatronic dinosaur displays twice, Bristol is currently having their third one and London zoo is having its first this summer - if I have counted correctly. They are popular with visitors, particularly with children (after all if they are interested in animals, they are very likely to be interested in dinosaurs too), and they are easy to install, relatively cheap to hire, with very low running costs and lots of merchandise to sell as well. You can understand why they are so popular with zoo managers." [16]

ENDNOTES

1   Downloaded on 3.2.2020 from https://lanterncompany.co.uk/chester-zoo-lantern-magic/
2   Downloaded on 3.2.2020 from https://lanterncompany.co.uk/what-we-do/
3   Downloaded on 3.2.2020 from https://www.tripadvisor.co.uk/ShowUserReviews-g186233-d213872-r147562450-Chester_Zoo-Chester_Cheshire_England.html
4   Downloaded of 3.2.2020 from https://www.cheshire-live.co.uk/news/chester-cheshire-news/chester-zoo-releases-extra-tickets-6404303
5   Downloaded on 3.2.2020 from https://www.tripadvisor.co.uk/ShowUserReviews-g186233-d213872-r243036716-Chester_Zoo-Chester_Cheshire_England.html
6   Downloaded on 3.2.2020 from https://www.cheshire-live.co.uk/whats-on/family-kids-news/lantern-magic-chester-zoo-christmas-10249793
7   Downloaded on 3.2.2020 from https://lanterncompany.co.uk/chester-zoo-lantern-magic-2015/
8   Downloaded on 3.2.2020 from https://www.liverpoolecho.co.uk/whats-on/family-kids-news/chester-zoos-christmas-lanterns-opened-12234556
9   Downloaded on 3.2.2020 from https://ultimate-uk.com/work/chester-zoo-lanterns-2017-creative-campaign/
10   Downloaded on 3.2.2020 from

https://www.cheshire-live.co.uk/whats-on/family-kids-news/review-chester-zoo-lanterns-parade-15491506

11   Downloaded on 3.2.2020 from
https://www.bbc.co.uk/newsround/23368476

12   Downloaded on 3.2.2020 from
https://www.cheshire-live.co.uk/news/chester-cheshire-news/giant-bugs-exhibition-chester-zoo-5314600

13   Downloaded on 3.2.2020 from
https://www.chesterzoo.org/news/predators/

14   Downloaded on 3.2.2020 from
https://www.manchestereveningnews.co.uk/whats-on/family-kids-news/predators-chester-zoo-guide-tickets-16323171

15   Downloaded on 3.2.2020 from
https://www.zoochat.com/community/threads/animatronic-animals-in-zoos-not-dinosaurs.292952/

16   Downloaded on 3.2.2020 from
https://www.zoochat.com/community/threads/dinosaur-exhibits-in-zoos.467084/

CHAPTER 9 VISITOR ATTRACTIONS

It is a matter for debate whether a zoo should focus strictly on animals and conservation, or whether it should also attempt to maximise visitor numbers and entertain its guests with the kind of rides and other attractions found in amusement parks such as Disneyland, Thorpe Park, Alton Towers and the Bear Grills Experience.

One might argue that zoos should "stick to the knitting" and not try, sometimes not very successfully, to emulate elements of an amusement park.

Initially the visitor attractions which were not strictly animal focused served some other purpose, such as facilitating guests' movement around the zoo.

An example of this was the monorail transportation system. The Liverpool Echo reported in September 2019, under the headline, 'Chester Zoo is scrapping its monorail after 28 years', "the popular Zoofari monorail, which first opened in 1991, has given rides to millions of visitors since it launched, offering views of the animals, habitats and gardens that call Chester Zoo home. But zoo bosses say the system 'doesn't even cover half' of the 125 acres of the tourist attraction, so have made the decision to take down the monorail later this summer."

The statement went on to say: "It has been part of the zoo for nearly three decades but since its installation in 1991 the zoo has grown in size and the transportation system now doesn't even cover half of the 125 acres. Over the last few years we have experienced both system and train failures, so this once state-of-the-art system is proving costly to maintain and unreliable for visitors."

The monorail, which was officially opened by the Duchess of Kent, even broke down on its first ever trip around the zoo - though has since played host to the likes of the Queen and Gary Barlow.

The monorail was built and installed by Computerised People Mover International at a cost of $4 million and then opened by the Duchess of Kent in 1991. The system was 1 mile (1½ km) long and travelled on an elevated guideway to give views of the park grounds – the track crossed Flag Lane twice on its one-way circular route. The two halves of the park were connected by the system and there was one station in each part, one near the lion enclosure (Jubilee Square station) and one near the monkey building (Tsavo station, formerly known as Monkey Island Station). Each train on the system could seat 24 passengers between its four cars and a full tour took around fifteen minutes.

According to Wikipedia, "The system is a straddle beam monorail. The layout has a separate depot and control room and carries approximately 2,000 passengers per day. T&M Machine Tool Electronics made improvements totaling £300,000 to the monorail's drive system and electrics in 2009, including more than 25 miles of new cabling.

Photo: Jeff Buck / Approaching the Elephant Bridge at Chester Zoo / CC BY-SA 2.0

The monorail was re-launched by music producer Pete Waterman during a visit on 23 July 2009, when Waterman drove the first loop of the new system. The upgraded system uses pairs of 2.2-kilowatt (3 hp) AC motors for each carriage, with remote monitoring managed over a 5Ghz wireless link. One week later a power failure occurred, requiring the first eight visitors of the day to be escorted off the monorail using a hydraulic lift.

In May 2012, Queen Elizabeth II and the Duke of

Edinburgh took a tour of the zoo in a specially redecorated monorail set painted in a Union Flag theme for her Diamond Jubilee." [2]

They then split up as the Queen was taken to see the rhino paddock while the Duke was taken to see the elephants. The Queen was greeted by two rhinos who were resting on some hay. She asked the keeper if they were 'keeping warm' and was then told about the zoo's breeding programme. The 40-minute tour was rounded off when Ruby Pilgrim, nine, presented the Queen with a posy. Ruby, daughter of the zoo's director general Dr Mark Pilgrim, said meeting the queen was exciting: "She asked me if I liked ponies and seeing the birds and animals in the zoo."

Dr Pilgrim said: "To have her majesty the Queen and the Duke of Edinburgh join us on this most special of days, and in her majesty's special year, is fantastic and a wonderful testament to what we are achieving through our passionate and dedicated staff." [3]

During the 2018 and 2019 seasons I received some training from experienced Guest Experience staff on how to operate the monorail, although I never quite achieved the proficiency level needed to get signed off as a qualified operator. Two sets of skills were involved – issuing tickets and actually operating the ride. Although there were four sets of carriages, usually only two were in operation at any one time. You had to direct guests to a queue, check that it was safe to open and close the doors and then press the button to send it off to the next station. One incident stuck in my memory: having to clean one of the compartments after a child had been sick all over the floor and doors. Fortunately, there was a magical spray you could use which removed the smell and caused the vomit to congeal into a sand-like substance, which could then easily be swept up with a dustpan and brush.

Today we said goodbye to the trains for good. Had the privilege of the chance to be on the last ever train that went round the track and come into the shed one last time with some great friends. Even had the chance to turn the last train off in memory of a very good friend who would have loved to have been a part of today 💜💜💜

Photos: Lauren Roberts

Treetop challenge replaced a mini-golf course in mid-2018. I'd like to think that this might have been inspired by its adult big brother, the high ropes and zip wires at the

Another 2 of the people who made the monorail special

Photo: Geraint Roberts

Bear Grills Adventure at the NEC in Birmingham, scaled down to suit 2 to 7-year olds!

The zoo website proclaims, "Bring your mini monkeys along to the zoo for a *big* adventure on our adventure course! Add even more excitement to your day at the zoo by bringing your little ones along to Treetop Challenge, the UK's biggest course of its type! Get them strapped into a harness and guide them around the many fun obstacles along the course. This course will have them monkeying around as they leap, balance, climb and laugh their way round. It's also the first course in the UK to include TWO mini zip lines, so you can watch your little ones wizzzz along!" [4] Parents are advised that it will take around 30 minutes to complete the course and children must be accompanied by an adult on the ground – as they will explore the different elements of the course together.

Not many reviews of Treetop Challenge have appeared to date. One reviewer on TripAdvisor says, "The treetop challenge was brilliant for our 6-year-old; she loved it. Well worth the extra £5 and you are able to follow them round on the journey. Well done Chester zoo!" [5]

Boat trips have been a feature of Chester zoo since the end of the 1950s when a canal system with water buses was established. The zoo opened Islands at Chester Zoo in July 2015, a project extending the footprint of the zoo by 15 acres and built to the south of the west half of the current site. Islands showcases areas where the zoo is involved in conservation programmes, including Sumatra, the Philippines and Indonesia.

Visitors are able to walk between the islands via a series of bridges and also view the animals via the Lazy River Boat Trip. Gareth Simpson, the zoo's operations implementation manager, explained that the project had its challenges: "Installing the boat cable is one of many, many challenging tasks we've already tackled on this exciting, but incredibly complex, project. The team from the zoo battled the elements, deep mud and high water to lay the cable. Such is the level of expertise needed on this project, an expert from Germany, who has worked with cable cars,

then joined us to advise on how to connect it all up to the mechanical wheels. The 14 boats that will be towed by the cable weigh over 11 tonnes and can carry up to 238 visitors at any one time, so installing it was no mean feat. I'm pleased to say that it's all now starting to come together nicely, and we can't wait for June." [6]

According to Intamin, the German firm which supplied the boats, the Tow Boat Ride is an attractive and relaxing boat ride constructed around an existing or man-made body of water. The attachment to the main drive cable gives the boats limited freedom of movement, creating the impression of free-floating boats. The installation operates without noise because of its drive system and is environmentally friendly. A few inches below the surface of the water is a steel wire rope, suspended by underwater deflection pulleys located at each desired turn. The Tow Boat Ride is an efficient and attractive amusement and transportation facility. [7]

When the ride first opened there were some very perceptive comments on Zoo Chat: [8]

'ChesterZooFan' asked, "With no canopy what will happen if it rains? I'm thinking more of the seats getting wet, having to be dried off every time before subsequent passengers board...."

'Gentle Lemur' (Alan) gave a very detailed description of what could be seen from the boat ride from the visitor's perspective. [9]

The Lazy River Boat Trip is a leisurely way of viewing the outdoor exhibits on the Islands which complements walking around the paths. When the Islands were first opened the paths were dusty when dry and muddy when wet, and it was soon realised that it was necessary to concrete them. From the perspective of keeping them tidy,

especially during autumn when there are leaves falling all the time, it would have been better if the paths had a smooth surface which could easily be brushed, as keeping them swept is something of a nightmare, as leaves get stuck all the time in the uneven surface. But aesthetically having an uneven surface looks more attractive! Guests approaching the boat jetty arrive at a covered entrance where there is a map of the route the boats take with details of the animals which can be seen at each point around the route. On busy days a member of the Guest Experience team stands at the "top of the queue" to warn parents of babes in arms that they will not be allowed on the boats unless their offspring can walk unaided, and to direct disabled visitors to head down the exit path towards the end of the jetty where disabled passengers can board, either under their own steam or in a wheelchair which is secured in place with ropes.

When you get close to the boat jetty there is a roof to keep the sun off, and a couple of barrows with imitation fruits typically found in Indonesia (mangoes, melons, bananas etc). There is a buggy park at the back of the jetty with cctv to ensure nobody messes with the pushchairs, while three of the boats currently in use can take disabled passengers in a wheelchair with their carer and the rest of their group.

When the boat ride was first commissioned, up to eighteen people were allowed onto each boat, with up to three on each of the six seats. There were fourteen boats on the continuous loop, which meant one had to leave the boat jetty just over once a minute, then it took fifteen minutes (assuming there were no stops to load disabled passengers onto a boat) before arriving back at the boat jetty.

According to 'Gentle Lemur', "The whole point of the Lazy River Trip is to sit back, relax and look around. We get a nice view of the Coral Sands area where we entered Islands. Then we arrive at the first warty pig beach. On our real trip the pigs were elsewhere. I presume that the branches are to indicate to the pigs that there is a barrier to prevent them going into the water. As the boat rounded the little headland between the warty pig beaches, I was impressed by the realism of the simulated riverbank. We were lucky enough to see two of the pigs on the second beach."

Coral Sands is nowadays where the boats currently out of use are beached, along with a typical wooden dugout canoe and various other artefacts. From here the boats pass under a bridge behind the Tree Kangaroo enclosure towards Papua, where they pass behind the Dusky Padmelons and then along the edge of the cassowary enclosure.

Beyond this is the banteng enclosure, which features a huge pool, slightly below the level of the river, before bending to the left around the mound on which the Balinese aviary is built.

Coming up on the right after the Lantern Bridge which links Bali and Sumatra is the tiger enclosure which has a very solid-looking wire fence. The tigers have a large enclosure which includes an off-show indoor area and two extensive grassy enclosures linked by a bridge over the pathway. This means that if visitors don't manage to see them from the boat there is a good chance they will come across them basking in the sun by following the path.

From here the boats bend round towards the Monsoon

Forest on the right, with its plastic roof currently being replaced following the 2019 fire.

Towards the end of the ride the boats pass under the Rock Bridge with a good view of the anoa paddock, ahead and to the right. There is a sharp bend which brings the boats around the corner and back to the boat jetty.

For most of 2019 the female anoa shared the paddock with her son, but once he reached maturity the risk of incest became too much and he was moved on to another zoo!

Most visitors are happy to sit back and enjoy the ride as they travel slowly and silently around the exhibits, looking at them from a different perspective. As 'Gentle Lemur' remarks, "Of course, you can't stop if you see something interesting and there can be no guarantee of seeing any animals at all, even when all the exhibits are complete and fully stocked. But all zoo nerds know that already and they will find plenty to interest them in the planting and design of the enclosures and the waterway."

Some modifications have been made to the original design of the boats, including adding a canopy to keep the rain off.

During the 2019 season the majority of my shifts were on the boats. Watching the cctv and controlling boat movements was reserved for permanent zoo staff, so as temporary staff we were assigned to either the front end of the boat jetty, loading passengers on to the boats or the back end, where they disembarked. On very busy days someone would also be assigned to the top of the queue at the start of the path down to the boat jetty. At the front of the jetty we would direct passengers to one of four rows, warn them to mind their heads and mind the gap, then give a little speech telling them to stay seated at all times, not rock the boat from side to side, not put arms or legs into the water and not to worry if the boat stopped for a few minutes – it would start again of its own accord. We then pushed the boat beyond the end of the jetty where it engaged with the cable and moved forward under its own steam. At the back end of the jetty it was a case of warning passengers to stay seated till the boat stopped, and to mind their head and mind the gap on leaving the boat. We had a wheelchair for disabled visitors, who could either board the boat using their own wheelchair or use the zoo wheelchair (electrically driven wheelchairs were not allowed onto the boats). Three of the boats had a removable plank to allow a ramp to be moved into place, then the wheelchair was secured with ropes to stop it moving about.

When the ride was first introduced, there were 14 boats which meant one had to leave the jetty every minute. Each boat had six seats, so assuming there were three passengers to a seat the maximum number per boat was 18. However, this frequency did not allow for any delays in loading and unloading, so several boats were removed, leaving eight, with a frequency of one every couple of minutes.

Parents of small babies sometimes objected when told their baby had to be capable of walking on and off the boat and wondered why they couldn't just be carried on board and sit on the grownup's knee. We had to explain that this wasn't just some arbitrary rule – it was for their own safety and it was part of the rules of the inspection scheme administered by ADIPS (the Amusement Devices Inspection Procedures Scheme). According to the ADIPS website, "Fairgrounds and amusement parks are relatively safe when compared with other leisure activities and, in fact, represent some of the safest leisure activities of all. Each year inspections are carried out by an independent ride inspection body, whose capability to perform competent and independent inspection is assessed and monitored on an ongoing basis under the ADIPS scheme." Most visitors accepted the rules but occasionally someone could get quite abusive and had to be sweet-talked until they calmed down.

Each year the zoo organises training for Guest Experience staff assigned to the boats in how to paddle a canoe in order to rescue stranded passengers in the event that a boat comes off the cable. In 2019 this took place after hours on a number of very cold days in autumn.

Another tough task was clearing the channel of the weed which grows profusely in the boat channel.

A further aspect of recent developments at the zoo is the creation of animal-themed play areas for children. The most recent of these is the Madagascar play area project supervised by BCA Landscape and completed in 2017. The zoo website declares, "There's sooooooo much to discover in our brand-new Play! space that's been lovingly created by our play experts.

Paddling a boat back to the boat jetty

Climb like a lemur and uncover our tree-top hideaways in the Lost Forest, crawl across the scramble nets like an aye-aye and play on our sandy beach like a ploughshare tortoise! (Animal impressions encouraged.) Make a BIG splash in our dry riverbed or play hide and seek in our Madagascar grasses. There's even chance to explore our Madagascar basecamp and find other surprises to discover." [10]

Another new play area is the Wildlife Wood. This replaced the "Fun Ark" which had outlived its day. The Fun Ark was a large timber and wood play area based on

Noah's Ark which catered for both 3 to 5-year olds and 6-to14-year olds in two separate sections. It included scramble ladders, crawl nets and adventure walkways and even a slide. Another play area which has been demolished was Little Acorns, for 3-12-year olds which featured two towers of fun that are reached by scramble nets and rope bridges. Once you were up there you could come down using the slide.

Removing weed from the boats channel

According to the zoo website, "the Wildlife Wood play area is inspired by our incredible UK wildlife and the amazing wildlife that can be found right here on our doorstep. Wildlife Wood features exciting and immersive zones that are all themed around local species and the zoo's Wildlife Connections campaign. Discover dens, slides, climbing ropes as well as a wildlife wheel that plays animal sounds."[11] The play area was designed by Timberplay, who say, "Most recently Timberplay worked with Chester Zoo last year on the creation of Wildlife Wood, an impressive combination of equipment designed to unleash the inner adventurer. The main hefty structure features generous timbers and comprises many elements, including a Climbing Forest combined with a three-tier triangular net configuration. This in turn, connects via a net tunnel to a special single-footed tree house, net tunnels and huge steel tunnel slide. Presented as a comprehensive unit, children can tackle the piece as a whole, plotting their way from one end to the other, or cherry pick the elements they want to conquer. With several levels of challenge within each element, children of all ages can find the appropriate element for their own physical ability. Wildlife Woods also includes several wheelchair accessible products, including a slide designed to be easily accessed by a wheelchair user, and also, the thrilling wheelchair see-saw, which has been uniquely incorporated as a bridge element. The wooded play area uses wood chip as its safety surface, offering a very natural feel, perfect for the wider zoo environment." [12]

ENDNOTES

1   Downloaded on 5.2.2020 from
https://www.liverpoolecho.co.uk/whats-on/whats-on-news/chester-zoos-monorail-being-scrapped-16494055

2   Downloaded on 5.2.2020 from
https://en.wikipedia.org/wiki/Chester_Zoo

3   Downloaded on 5.2.2020 from
https://www.dailymail.co.uk/femail/article-2145240/Your-carriages-await-Maam-Brave-Queen-cruises-Mersey-duck-rides-monorail-Chester-Zoo-Diamond-Jubilee-tour.html

4   Downloaded on 5.2.2020 from
https://www.chesterzoo.org/whats-here/treetop-challenge/

5   Downloaded on 5.2.2020 from
https://www.tripadvisor.co.uk/ShowUserReviews-g186233-d213872-r649693602-Chester_Zoo-Chester_Cheshire_England.html

6   Downloaded on 5.2.2020 from
https://blooloop.com/news/chester-zoo-islands-lazy-river-boat-ride-progress/

7   Downloaded on 7.2.2020 from
https://www.intaminworldwide.com/project/lazy-river-boat-trip/

8   Downloaded on 7.2.2020 from
https://www.zoochat.com/community/media/islands-lazy-river-cruise-boats.297641/?page=2

9   Downloaded on 7.2.2020 from

10 THE SECRET LIFE OF THE ZOO

"The Secret Life of the Zoo" is a remarkably successful documentary programme produced by Blast! Films on behalf of Channel 4. The series is filmed on location at Chester Zoo, and focuses on the behaviour of the animals at the zoo and their relationships with the keepers. The first five series were narrated by Olivia Colman. Actress Tamsin Greig took over narration from the sixth series. A seventh series has just been broadcast and a further two series are currently being planned.

I was thrown in at the deep end, as there was a party to celebrate the launch of the latest series of the Secret Life of the Zoo at the nearby Hilton Hotel the evening after I had finished my very first day working at the zoo, with champagne and cocktails followed by a showing of an episode from the latest series. I arrived quite late as the satnav took me off in completely the wrong direction.

When I posted a picture of the party on Facebook, one of the comments I got from my friends was "Working - really???"

Survived my first day working at Chester Zoo, ending up with a staff party, drinking champagne, watching the latest episode of The Secret Life of the Zoo live on a big screen and meeting the Producer..... — at DoubleTree by Hilton (Chester, Cheshire)

The series gives viewers behind the scenes access to the zoo's 21,000 animals and includes numerous shots of keepers in action and short interviews with the people who work there. The zoo's keepers are interviewed in each episode about the various animals and incidents.

The production company Blast Films! called on the expertise of rig specialist Minicams to help it get up close and personal to the animals in a bid to show the lives of the animals as never before. [1]

"We wanted the animals to be the protagonists and to be able to tell the story from their perspective, which meant not having the bars of cages in shot," says Blast! head of programmes Nick Hornby. "The only way to do that was to put cameras in the cages, which meant using fixed cameras. And we wanted the shows to include a broad range of animals, so we needed to be able to move in and out of different enclosures."

Blast! turned to Minicams, and used a technique described as guerrilla filming.

"Rather than a large-scale, 100 camera set-up, we provided a small unit with a single operator who could move around and install cameras, cables and other kit where and when required," says Minicams managing director Nick McLachlan. "With tapeless, you can start recording in the morning and let it run in the background, or all night with infrared cameras. Then you simply hand all the footage to production on one drive," says McLachlan. [2]

The first series was filmed over 10 months and attracted an average of 2.5 million viewers for each of its six episodes. Wikipedia summarised the content of each episode: [2]

1   Asian elephant Thi-Hi-Way gives birth to female calf, Nandita. Asian small clawed otters Daisy and Robbie are retiring from the breeding program. Red pandas Jung and Nima have cubs and the Chimpanzees are fighting for dominance.

2   The keepers face the challenge of moving a family of five rare Sumatran tigers to a brand-new enclosure. The Montserrat Tarantulas are set up on a date. Sun bears Milli and Toni join the collection from the Rare Species Conservation Centre in Kent.

3   Rothschild's giraffe Orla gives birth to a male calf

named Kidepo. The keepers attempt to breed from the critically endangered Mountain Chicken Frogs.

4   Florence the Grevy's Zebra arrives from the West Midland Safari Park to meet resident stallion, Mac. The elephant house is hit by a potentially deadly virus with two of the babies Hari and Bala falling gravely ill.

5   The Humboldt penguin chicks are introduced to the main pool. Two new Sunda Gharial Crocodiles arrive from France but refuse to eat. Boris the Chimpanzee takes a wild Moorhen chick hostage and keepers try to work out why two Bornean River Turtles are not breeding.

6   Female Black rhinoceros Kitani is introduced to potential mate, Magadi. A baby Sumatran orangutan is born

The series received very favourable press reviews. Gerard O'Donovan of The Daily Telegraph stated "For those who like their nature full of cute oohs and aahs, rather than red in tooth and claw, The Secret Life of the Zoo gently ticked all the boxes."[3] O'Donovan's colleague Michael Hogan gave the opening episode of the fourth series a positive review, saying that it made him "emotionally invested as the devoted zookeepers." [4] He found the "gently joyful documentary" was made all the more "uplifting" thanks to Colman's narration. He concluded, "it might have been no Blue Planet II, but The Secret Life of the Zoo was equally enchanting in its own, more modest way." [5]

The Daily Express described the very first episode in January 2016 at some length:

"In this week's first episode we witness the uplifting sight of an Asian elephant, 34-year-old Thi Hi Way, giving birth to a female calf after a 22-month gestation, and a male chimp, Eric, fighting pack leader Dylan for dominance, which results in injury for Dylan. And after eight years, the zoo's dominant pair of otters, Daisy and Robbie, are moved on to retirement to make way for a new breeding pair.

We see zookeeper Kirsten Wicks, 26, trying to round up eight-week-old meerkats so they can be checked and microchipped. Although it's not as difficult as interacting with dangerous wild beasts, it's still not easy.

The meerkats, she explains, are pack animals that guard each other closely. "As soon as you take one of the babies in your hand the rest of the meerkat mob go from being your best friend, the person who feeds them, to them hating you and wanting to kill you," she explains.

"I've had the dad meerkat hanging off my shin and it hurts. But that's just what nature tells him to do to protect his child." [6]

One of the things I really liked about this series was that it enabled you to find out the names of all the various animals and other creatures featured in each episode. By and large the zoo tends not to publicise the names of most of the animals, apart from the larger mammals. So, whilst there are posters and billboards with the names of the elephants, sloths, jaguars, giant otters and orangutans dotted around the zoo, you won't find the names of many of the smaller creatures on any of the zoo's publicity materials or the zoo website. When I first started working at the zoo, I used to watch each episode of the Secret Life of the Zoo and jot down the names of the key animals, creating my own Who's Who of the Zoo.

It seems an eminently sensible policy not to widely publicise the names of the smaller animals, birds and fish, as it would be virtually impossible to keep the list of names up to date. Even in the short time I have worked at the zoo many examples of endangered species have been transferred to other zoos, or sadly have passed away, whilst new babies appear almost daily.

ENDNOTES

1   Downloaded on 11.2.2020 from https://www.broadcastnow.co.uk/behind-the-scenes-the-secret-life-of-the-zoo/5101096.article

2   ibid

3   Downloaded on 11.2.2020 from https://www.telegraph.co.uk/tv/2016/11/17/secrets-of-the-zoo-gently-ticks-all-the-boxes-with-nature-full-o/

4   Downloaded on 11.2.2020 from https://www.telegraph.co.uk/tv/2017/11/15/secret-life-zoo-makes-compelling-cockle-warming-viewing-review/

5   ibid

6   Downloaded on 11.2.2020 from https://www.express.co.uk/life-Season 8Zoo

CHAPTER 11 KEEPING THE STAFF HAPPY

The Guest Experience team in both zones where I have worked since the start of 2017 were a happy bunch. During the year there were various occasions when everyone could get together and let their hair down.

The zoo party at Rosie's 8th September 2017

One of these was the "end of season party," which took place in September shortly before most of the seasonal staff were due to finish their contracts and return to studying or other pursuits.

Zoo party at Off the Wall

These were usually held at Rosies or Off the Wall, but in 2019 the venue switched to the Commercial Hotel.

In December 2020 we all got a bottle of Chester Zoo gin to mark the occasion when the zoo had 2 million visitors for the first time during the course of a year.

In the run-up to Christmas each year there was a celebratory meal in the staff canteen or Bembe restaurant.

Occasionally staff who were leaving for another job or moving to another zone would invite friends to join them at the Wheatsheaf (affectionately known as "Zone 4") or some other venue to celebrate their departure, then post pictures on Facebook or other social media.

Celebrating the 2 millionth visitor to the zoo

Lovely evening drinks at the Wheatsheaf this evening
😊 going to miss the staff at CZ. Sorry i can't say bye to
all of you individually 🩶

Emma's leaving do

Other popular pastimes included Bowling at Cheshire Oaks, Quiz Nights, and on one occasion Karting in Sandicroft.

End of Season party 29.11.2019

Karting with the Zone 2 Guest Experience team 26.6.2017 at Apex Kart, Chester

Each year most of the seasonal staff left at the end of August. One of the saddest things for me was getting to the end of the season and not knowing if you would ever again see people with whom you had shared the good times and the bad, laughter and sadness, dreams and delights.

CHAPTER 12 KEEPING THE ANIMALS HAPPY

Are we right to use animals as objects of entertainment, keeping them captive in zoos to entertain paying members of the public?

Increasingly zoos (and Chester is one of these) would argue that they are playing a vital role in the preservation of endangered species which are otherwise threatened with extinction. Indeed, some animals such as the New Guinea Singing Dog and Pinta Island Tortoise only exist in zoos and are now extinct in the wild. [1]

Grey (2017) points out that modern zoos generally apply the Five Freedoms originally developed by the British Farm Animal Welfare Council in 1979 and adopted by many animal welfare organisations. These are freedom from hunger and thirst, freedom from discomfort, freedom from pain, injury or disease, freedom to express normal behavior and freedom from fear and distress.

However, current shifts in welfare thinking recognize

positive welfare states ("freedom to", rather than "freedom from") and adopt a five domains model.[2] New Zealand Academic David Mellor has developed this to take account of internal body conditions and external environmental conditions which give rise to subjective experiences, allowing the welfare of an individual animal to be measured on a scale of good to bad. His model looks at five domains of potential welfare, nutrition, environment, health, behavior and mental state. Positive experiences in the domains lead to positive welfare states, and it is desirable to increase positive welfare states and reduce negative ones. [3]

In a Guardian article entitled "Why Zoos are Good", Dr David Hone argues that "it is perfectly possible to keep them in a zoo or wildlife park and for them to have a quality of life as high as, or higher than, in the wild. Their movement might be restricted (but not necessarily by that much) but they will not suffer from the threat or stress of predators (and nor will they be killed in a grisly manner or eaten alive) or the irritation and pain of parasites, injuries and illnesses will be treated, they won't suffer or die of drought or starvation and indeed will get a varied and high-quality diet with all the supplements required. They can be spared bullying or social ostracism or even infanticide by others of their kind, or a lack of a suitable home or environment in which to live. A lot of very nasty things happen to truly 'wild' animals that simply don't happen in good zoos and to cast a life that is 'free' as one that is 'good' is, I think, an error." [4]

In an earlier version of this article, Hone set out three key arguments in favour of zoos.

"But what do zoos actually bring to the table for the visitors and the wider world?

Education. Many children and adults, especially those in cities will never see a wild animal beyond a fox or pigeon, let alone a lion or giraffe. Sure documentaries get ever more detailed and impressive, and lots of things are on display in museums, but that really does pale next to seeing a living creature in the flesh, hearing it, smelling it, watching what it does and having the time to absorb details. That will bring a greater understanding and perspective to many and hopefully give them a greater appreciation for wildlife, conservation efforts and how they can contribute. That's before the actual direct education that can take place through signs, talks and the like that can directly communicate information about the animals they are seeing and their place in the world.

Conservation – reservoir and return. It's not an exaggeration that colossal numbers of species are going extinct across the world, and many more are threatened. Moreover, some of these collapses have been sudden, dramatic and unexpected or were simply discovered very late in the day. Zoos protect against a species going extinct. A species protected in captivity provides a reservoir population against a crash or extinction. Here they are relatively safe and can be bred up to provide foundation populations. A good number of species only exist in captivity and still more only exist in the wild because they have been reintroduced from zoos, or the wild populations have been boosted by captive bred animals. Quite simply without these efforts there would be fewer species alive today and ecosystems and the world as a whole would be poorer for it.

Research. If we are to save many wild species and restore and repair eco systems we need to know about how key species live, act and react. Being able to study animals in zoos where there is less risk and less variables means real changes can be effected on wild populations with far fewer problems. Knowing say the oestreus cycle of an animal or their breeding rate, or that they don't seem to like a crop that's about to be planted can make a real difference to conservation efforts and to reduce human-animal conflicts.

All in all, with the ongoing global threats to the environment it's hard for me to see zoos as anything other than being essential to the long-term survival of numerous species. Not just in terms of protecting them and breeding them for reintroduction, but to learn about them to aid those still in the wild, as well as to educate and inform the public about these animals and to pique their interest so that they can assist or at least accept the need to be more environmentally conscious. Sure there is always scope for improvement, but these benefits are critical to many species and potentially at least, the world as a whole, and the animals so well kept and content, that I think there can be few serious objections to the concept of zoos as a whole and what they can do. Without them, the world would be and would increasingly be, a poorer place." [5]

ENDNOTES

1   Downloaded on 24.02.2020 from
http://www.bbc.co.uk/ethics/animals/using/entertainment_1.shtml
2   Grey (2017) p 26
3   Mellor, D, quoted in Grey (2017), p 66
4   Downloaded on 24.02.2020 from
https://www.theguardian.com/science/lost-worlds/2014/aug/19/why-zoos-are-good
5   Downloaded on 24.02.2020 from
https://archosaurmusings.wordpress.com/2012/04/17/why-zoos-are-good/

CHAPTER 13 PREVENTING EXTINCTION

In the biblical account of creation, God tells Adam to "fill the earth and subdue it and have dominion over the fish of the sea and over the birds of the heavens and over every living thing that moves on the earth." (Genesis 1 v 28). With this power human beings have over all other living creatures comes a responsibility to ensure their continued survival - hence the Chester Zoo mission, "Preventing Extinction."

The zoo has a team of over forty experts working to protect wildlife. Their research focuses on six key regions around the globe and aims to understand the growing threats faced by wildlife. In early 2020 there were 66 ongoing conservation projects in 21 countries around the world.

According to the zoo website, "we use an evidence-based approach to help in the decision-making that improves the management of the animals and plants in our care, influences the sustainability of wildlife populations, and inspires the next generation of conservationists."

As the zoo continues to implement its strategic development plan, the regions where we focus on conservation will be represented in the different zones that visitors will experience on a visit to the zoo. The first of these zones, already complete, is Islands and represents the zoo's efforts to prevent the extinction of species in South-East Asia, and especially in The Philippines and Indonesia.

The focus is on six key specialisms:

1 *Livelihoods and sustainable development.*

Communities which live close to wildlife or protected areas need to see the benefits of conservation to be able to support it.

2 *Visitor and community engagement.*

A large part of the zoo's role is to engage many of the two million visitors each year in the conservation and protection of wildlife, raising awareness and educating the public so they can maximise their contribution to conservation.

3 *Wildlife health and wellbeing.*

The zoo regularly carries out research to improve the health and wellbeing of all the wildlife at the zoo, evaluating husbandry techniques, the habitat spaces and environmental enrichment. It investigates causes and treatments for diseases to benefit both animals at the zoo and their species in the wild.

4   *Conservation breeding and management.*

The zoo is a centre of excellence for conservation breeding and management, investigating factors which have a negative impact on reproductive success and maximizing the chances of captive bred individuals being successfully reintroduced to the wild.

5   *Human-wildlife conflict.*

Preventing and mitigating conflict requires an understanding of the movement and needs of the species and the underlying political cultural and economic factors underlying conflicts.

6   *Biodiversity surveys and ecological monitoring.*

These are key research tools which help define areas of greatest conservation value and need and provide data to monitor and evaluate the success of conservation measures implemented. The zoo website has details of staff qualifications and expertise, and of research projects with which the zoo is involved in each of the six specialisms.

Each year non-specialist permanent staff at the zoo are selected to go on short-term conservation trips to key sites overseas and in the UK, accompanying the professional experts.

If zoos in the 21st century are to survive criticism from organisations such as PETA, it is this focus on awareness-raising, conservation and preventing extinction which will ensure they continue to be a thriving force for good in the world, promoting the welfare and preservation of animals and educating humanity.

CHAPTER 14 DEALING WITH CORONAVIUS

Early in 2020 I took three months off in between seasonal contracts and spent much of the time researching and writing this book. In mid-March my 70th birthday was approaching and my family organised a magnificent celebratory meal for a group of family and friends at

Chester's Opera Grill. Little did we realise that just a week later the entire country would go into lockdown because of the outbreak of the Covid-19 coronavirus pandemic. In early March I had signed a seasonal contract running from 22nd March to early September, and I was all set to attend a training course for new and returning seasonal staff over the weekend of 21st and 22nd March.

However, this was not to be. A couple of days prior to the course there was a phone call from one of the zoo's senior managers to say that, because of the coronavirus outbreak, all new contracts for seasonal staff were being cancelled, although the zoo would still pay for any time already spend on online training courses.

Even if the contract hadn't been cancelled, I would have been unable to work as planned, having just turned 70, as all older people over the age of 70 were being advised to avoid all social contacts and maintain social distance, as the virus appeared to affect older people much more severely.

Six weeks later, I have binge-watched the entire horrific but hugely popular series "Tiger King" on Netflix, started the course reading to become a qualified Green Badge tour guide, and begun improving my Spanish, whilst only leaving the house once or twice a week for a brief raid on the local supermarket and once a day to walk the dog. And now we learn that over 70s may have to endure this enforced period of self-isolation for at least four months and possibly for up to a year!

Never before have we experienced the lockdown of

entire countries for weeks on end, the banning of all but essential travel, the closure of all forms of entertainment and leisure activities, including sports events, restaurants, pubs, cinemas, museums, churches and even parks and gardens, the shutting down of all but essential shops and services, and daily updates on tv on how far and how fast the virus has spread in the previous twenty four hours.

There have been major pandemics in the past. The Antonine Plague in AD 165-180 killed around 5 million people, the bubonic Plague of Justinian, spread by rats, (AD 541-2) killed over 25 million, while in the 14th century the Black Death killed between 70 and 100 million, or about 20% of the world's entire population. A flu pandemic at the end of World War I killed between 20 and 50 million. In addition, there have been frequent epidemics in the 21st century including AIDS, SARS and Ebola. Now people fear for their health, for their families and friends, especially the elderly and infirm, for their food supply, jobs, salaries, and even the availability of toilet paper.

At first the zoo carried on as usual. Cheshire Live reported on March 13th, "Chester Zoo is open as normal despite increased fears over the coronavirus in Cheshire and the UK. It's business as usual for the zoo which sees more than a million people enter its doors every year. Although cases of the coronavirus have risen, the zoo has said they are taking every precaution for staff, visitors and animals. The zoo's announcement comes after a number of events have already been cancelled in Cheshire over the

coronavirus. Animals have not been affected by the virus."
(1)

By this date (March 13th), there had been three confirmed cases involving Cheshire, in Chester, Macclesfield and Warrington. There were no cases or suspicions that animals could catch COVID-19.

Cheshire Live quoted a zoo spokesperson as saying, "COVID-19 is a brand new strain of coronavirus and global experts currently don't know everything about it in humans, let alone animals. The zoo is, of course, taking every precaution for staff, visitors and animals, but our expert animal teams have always had a strict set of biosecurity measures in place given that we're home to so many rare and precious species. In terms of visitors, the zoo is open as normal. With the continued worldwide concerns associated with the virus, and as a world-class organisation, the zoo is closely following the very latest Government and World Health Organisation advice." The article went on to say that the World Health Organisation had confirmed the coronavirus was now officially a pandemic. At Chester Zoo additional cleaning had been undertaken in public areas and staff were encouraging visitors to wash their hands thoroughly with soap and water on a regular basis.

"To make this as easy as possible for visitors, they'll find over 100 wash stations dotted around the zoo's 128 acres of zoological gardens," said a Chester Zoo spokesperson. "Since the incredibly and unusually wet February, visitor numbers have actually been slightly higher than we'd normally expect at this time of year - I think people are well aware of what a huge, open site the zoo is." [2]

The only occasion on which the zoo had previously been closed to visitors for extended periods was during an outbreak of foot and mouth disease. In 1968 the zoo was initially closed to the public for 11 weeks. The zoo website's "memories" section notes, "After a second spread of foot and mouth disease which forced the zoo to close for six weeks, the zoo re-opened over a weekend. The zoo made the decision to open to public, and very strict measures were put in place, including disinfectant foot-baths and all cars and vehicles were washed before they came on site. Our staff volunteered to work an extra day without pay to make sure the zoo could open to the public. And it was all hands on deck, as the day we opened, visitor numbers reached nearly 45,000!" [3]

On 17th March the zoo issued an update, stating that it was remaining open for visitors but following the previous day's announcement by the Government, restaurants and cafes at the zoo, including The Oakfield pub, would be closed. Takeaway food and drink outlets would stay open to provide refreshments for visitors but all teaching sessions and workshops, both off site and at the zoo would be cancelled for the time being. [4]

The zoo said in a statement, "During these difficult times, we continue to focus on the safety and welfare of our staff and visitors, while, of course, ensuring that the animals enjoy the exact same levels of care and attention they receive all year round. We also continue, from here in Chester, to fight for a better future for endangered animals all around the world."

However just a few days later on March 21st the Chester Standard reported that a new statement on the zoo website said: "Following Government advice on social distancing, Chester Zoo will close its gates to visitors for the foreseeable future, from 4.30pm today, Saturday, March 21. How long this will be for, we simply don't know, but we really hope it plays a part in slowing down the spread of this awful virus. Rest assured, that our incredibly dedicated animal experts, including zookeepers, vets and scientists will continue to ensure that the animals at the zoo enjoy the same levels of care and attention they receive all year round. Meanwhile, various other teams will be working from home and will continue fighting to give a brighter future for endangered species all around the world. With the continued worldwide concerns associated with coronavirus, the zoo is closely following the very latest Government and World Health Organisation (WHO) advice. As a world-class organisation we are, of course, taking every precaution for both staff and animals under our care. Our expert teams have always had a strict set of biosecurity measures in place given that we're home to so many rare and precious species. Our conservationists will continue to ensure that the animals enjoy the exact same levels of care and attention they receive all year round. Staff with underlying health conditions as well as those who are pregnant or over the age of 70 have been asked to stay home for the foreseeable future and take preventative measures as recommended by the Government and WHO." Among its frequently asked questions, the zoo added that all events scheduled until the end of May would not take place, and that Zoo members would receive a month's free membership, with that being potentially extended depending on how the pandemic took effect. Those with booked tickets could exchange these for open-dated tickets, which could be used any time later in the year once the zoo reopened. [5]

Meanwhile, the zoo has been organising virtual zoo days via its Facebook page. Day 5 began at 10.00 am with breakfast with the Red River Hog family, then lunch with the Painted Dog pack, a meeting with the cool Cassowary, followed by Reticulated Python snack time and ending with Chimpanzee feeding time. The final session of the day attracted almost 250,000 views.

The zoo has recently set up a "Just Giving" page to help cover its expenses whilst not receiving any income from visitors.

"Preventing extinction NEVER STOPS! And with over 35,000 threatened and critically endangered animals at Chester Zoo, our keepers and conservationists are still hard at work, come rain, hail or shine, making sure they all receive the same care and attention they enjoy all year round. Despite everything going on, our conservation experts will continue the fight to prevent extinction, and ensure a future for endangered species, no matter how big or how small.

Whilst we plan for as many eventualities as we possibly can, this situation we all find ourselves in is extraordinary. Visitor income is critical to us; it makes up about 97% of our income. Without being open, this certainly has its challenges, but whatever happens we'll continue to provide each and every animal with the same incredible care they receive all year round.

So many of you have asked how you can help, and the absolute best way you can do so right now is by making a small donation if you can, and allowing us to use it where we need it most. After all, it costs us a MASSIVE £465,000 a month simply to look after the animals and plants! These are difficult times for everyone, so make sure you and your family come first. After that, if the lack of your daily take-out coffee means you have a bit spare to donate to your favourite charities, then please do. Charities need your support more than ever.

And if that happens to be #TheZoo - amazing! [6]

ENDNOTES

1   Downloaded on 3.4.2020 from https://www.cheshire-live.co.uk/news/chester-cheshire-news/chester-zoo-open-operating-normal-17918972
2   ibid
3   Downloaded on 3.4.2020 from https://www.chesterzoo.org/memories/dedicated-staff-pull-together/
4   Downloaded on 3.4.3030 from

Spot the sloth! It didn't move between 1200 noon when I started work and 5.00 p.m. when I left!

Boris, Boats and Me

ABOUT THE AUTHOR

After a successful career as a British Council officer, Paul Woods was looking for a satisfying and rewarding retirement job. He found this as a seasonal Guest Experience Assistant at Chester Zoo, the UK's number one zoo and the third most popular zoo in the world. The challenge of helping in a very small way to create memorable experiences for some of the 2 million plus visitors to the zoo each year, encouraged him to leave behind the stresses and strains of a semi-diplomatic lifestyle and adapt to a physically rather than intellectually demanding job in a delightful environment. Paul is married to Fanta, and they have two grown-up children and a Labrador named Luna.

Printed in Great Britain
by Amazon